I'M SO PREGNANT

An illustrated look at the ups and downs
(and everything in between) of pregnancy

Line Severinsen

Adamsmedia
Avon, Massachusetts

Published by
Adams Media, a division of F+W Media, Inc.
57 Littlefield Street, Avon, MA 02322. U.S.A.
www.adamsmedia.com

ISBN 10: 1-5072-0186-9
ISBN 13: 978-1-5072-0186-2

Printed in China.

10   9   8   7   6   5   4   3   2   1

Many of the designations used by manufacturers and sellers to distinguish their products
are claimed as trademarks. Where those designations appear in this book and F+W Media,
Inc., was aware of a trademark claim, the designations have been printed with initial capital
letters.

Cover design by Stephanie Hannus.
Cover and interior illustrations by Line Severinsen.

This book is available at quantity discounts for bulk purchases.
For information, please call 1-800-289-0963.

Hi, I'm Line.

Like many women, when I became pregnant with my first baby, I was *so* excited to have the experience of carrying a child. I immediately started buying baby clothes and books and wipes and preparing our house for our little girl's arrival.

But then, not long into my first trimester, I started noticing how the media and blogosphere continuously painted pregnancy in such a glorious light, completely leaving out the negative things that many pregnant women experienced. It was all glowing skin and Lamaze breathing. What about the hellish heartburn, the terrifying mood swings, and having to pee every 5 minutes?

That's when I grabbed my pencils.

I wanted to tell my pregnancy story in an honest way, using humor to show the real ups and downs that come with carrying a baby. I had no idea so many women would embrace my work and find laughter and support in these comics. In the end, I like to think that these drawings show that while pregnancy is not always easy (or pretty, or comfortable, or fun), in the end, when you see your baby for the first time, it is *completely* worth it.

Congratulations! You're pregnant!

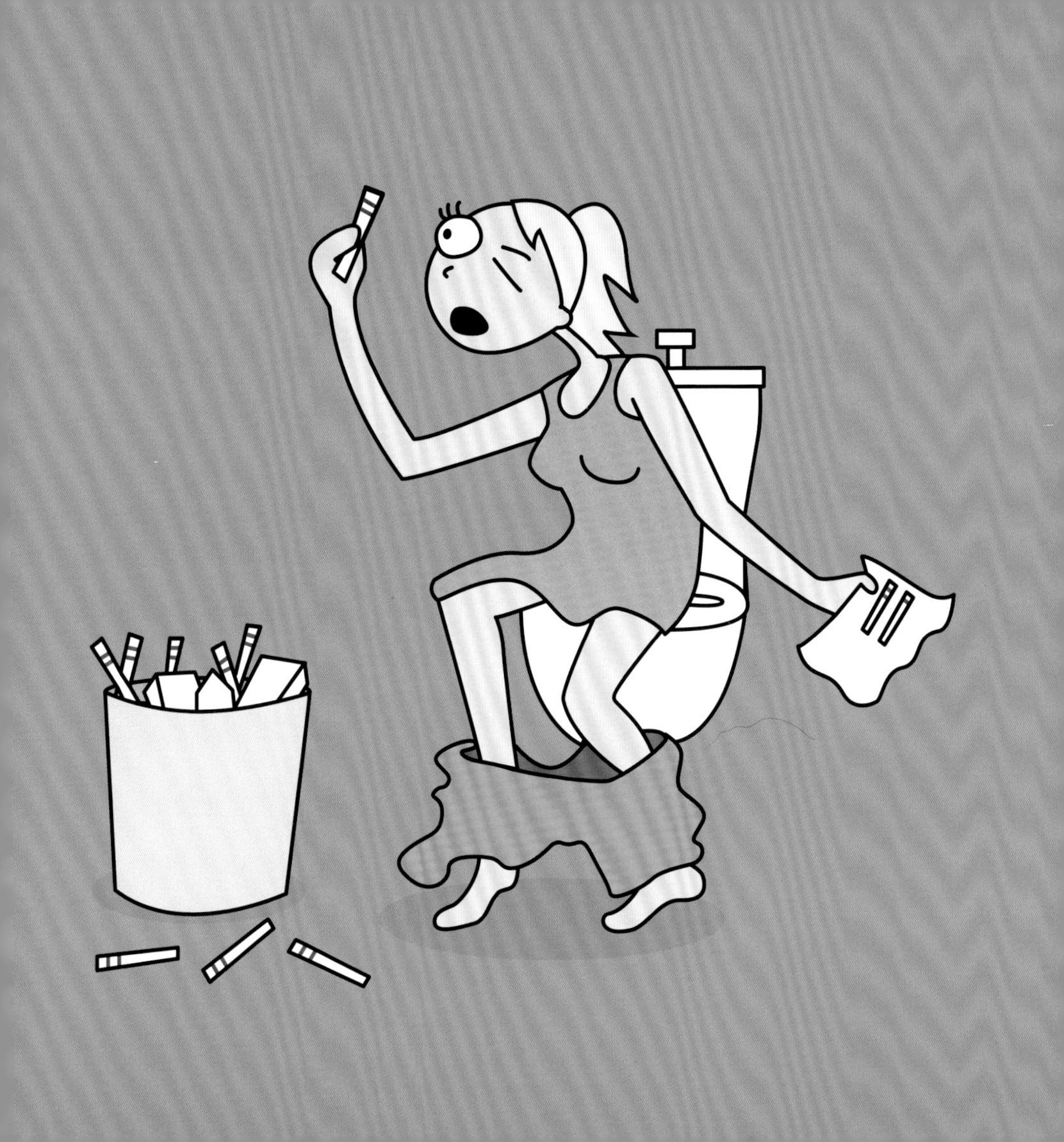

Surprise! We've got a bun in the oven.

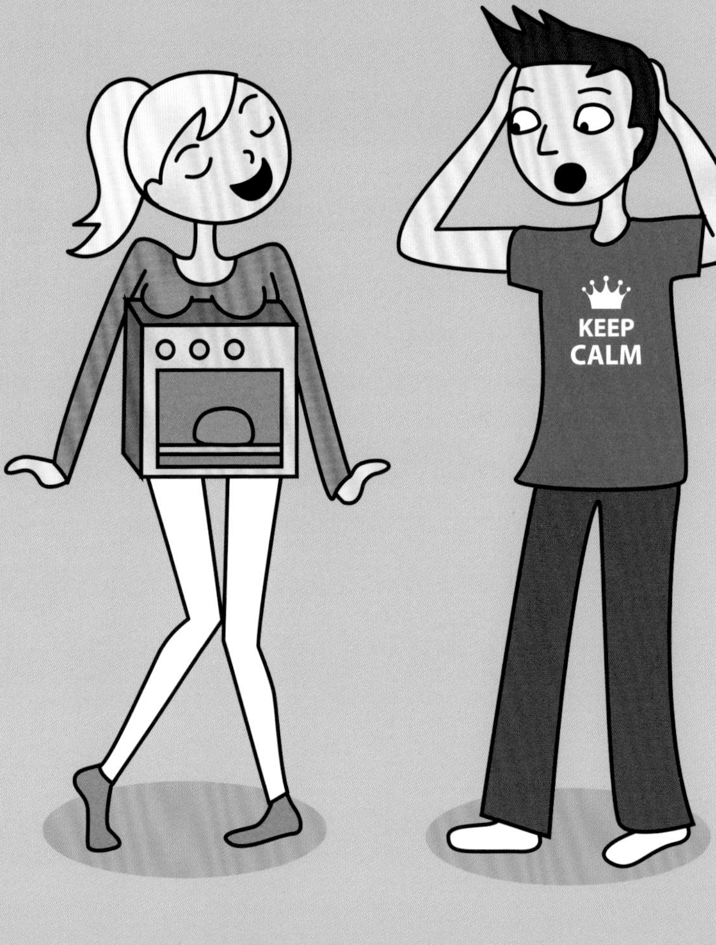
KEEP
CALM

Why do they call it morning sickness when it lasts all day?

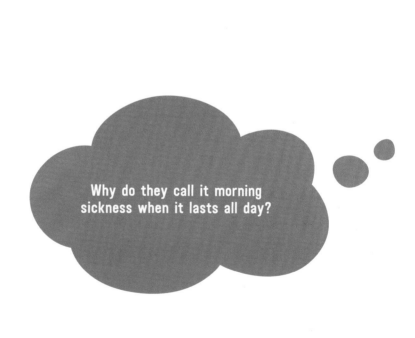

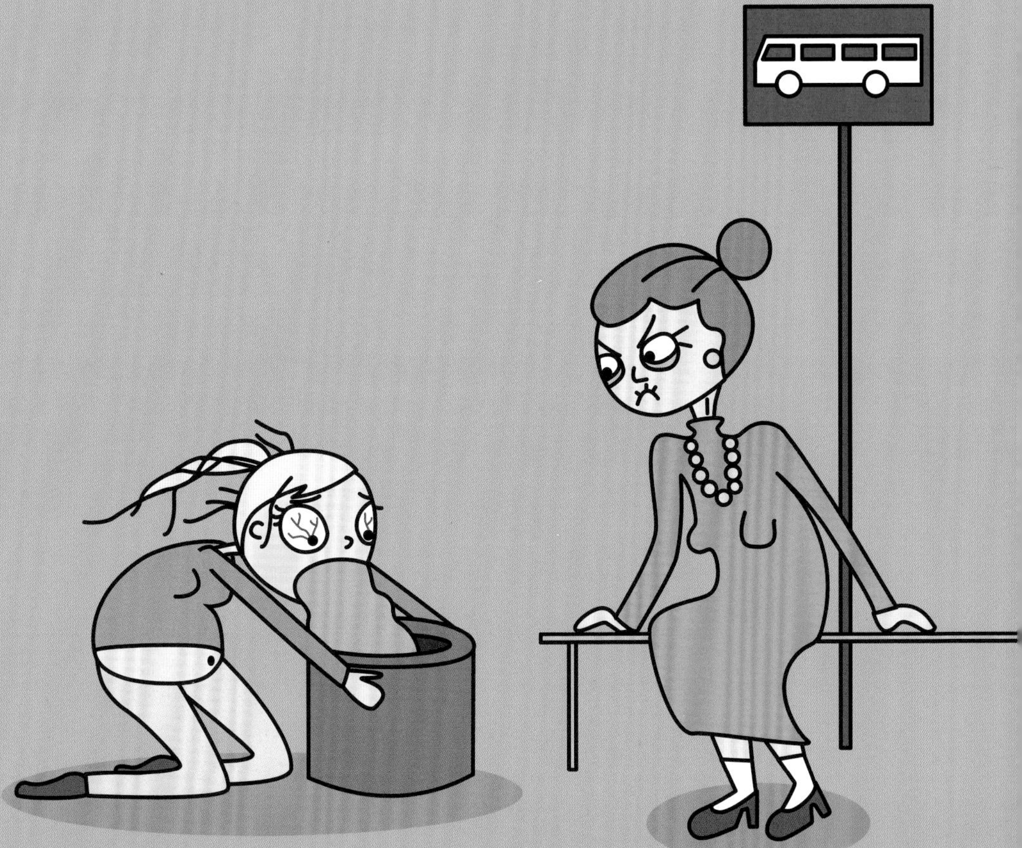

Another productive day at work.

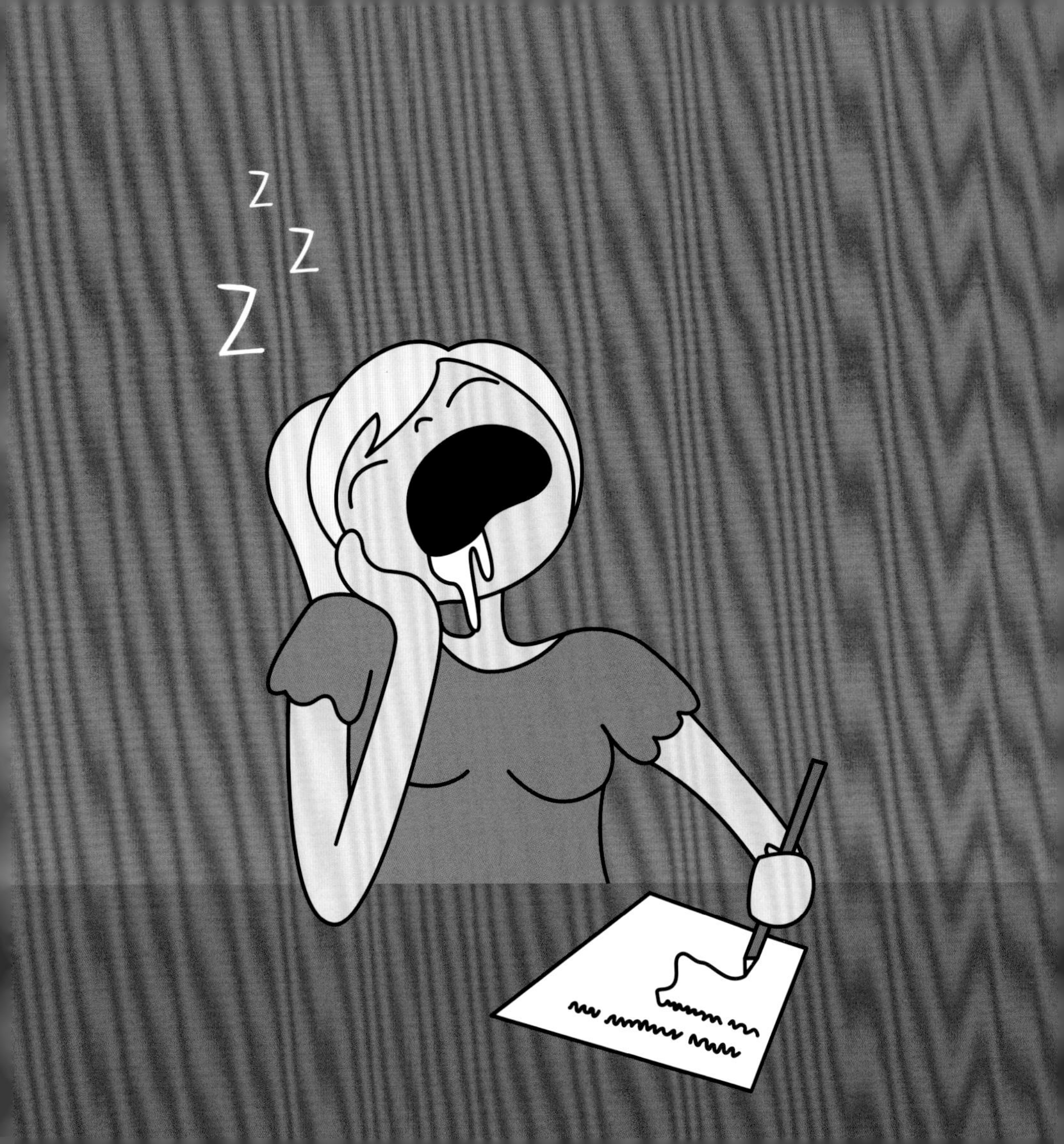
Z
Z
Z

I thought you were supposed to
"glow" when you're pregnant.

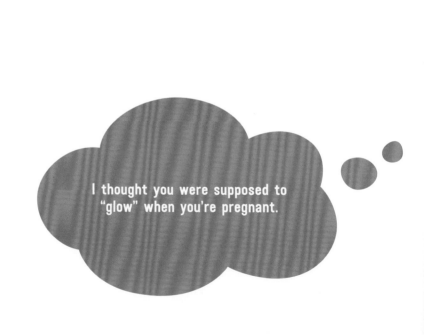

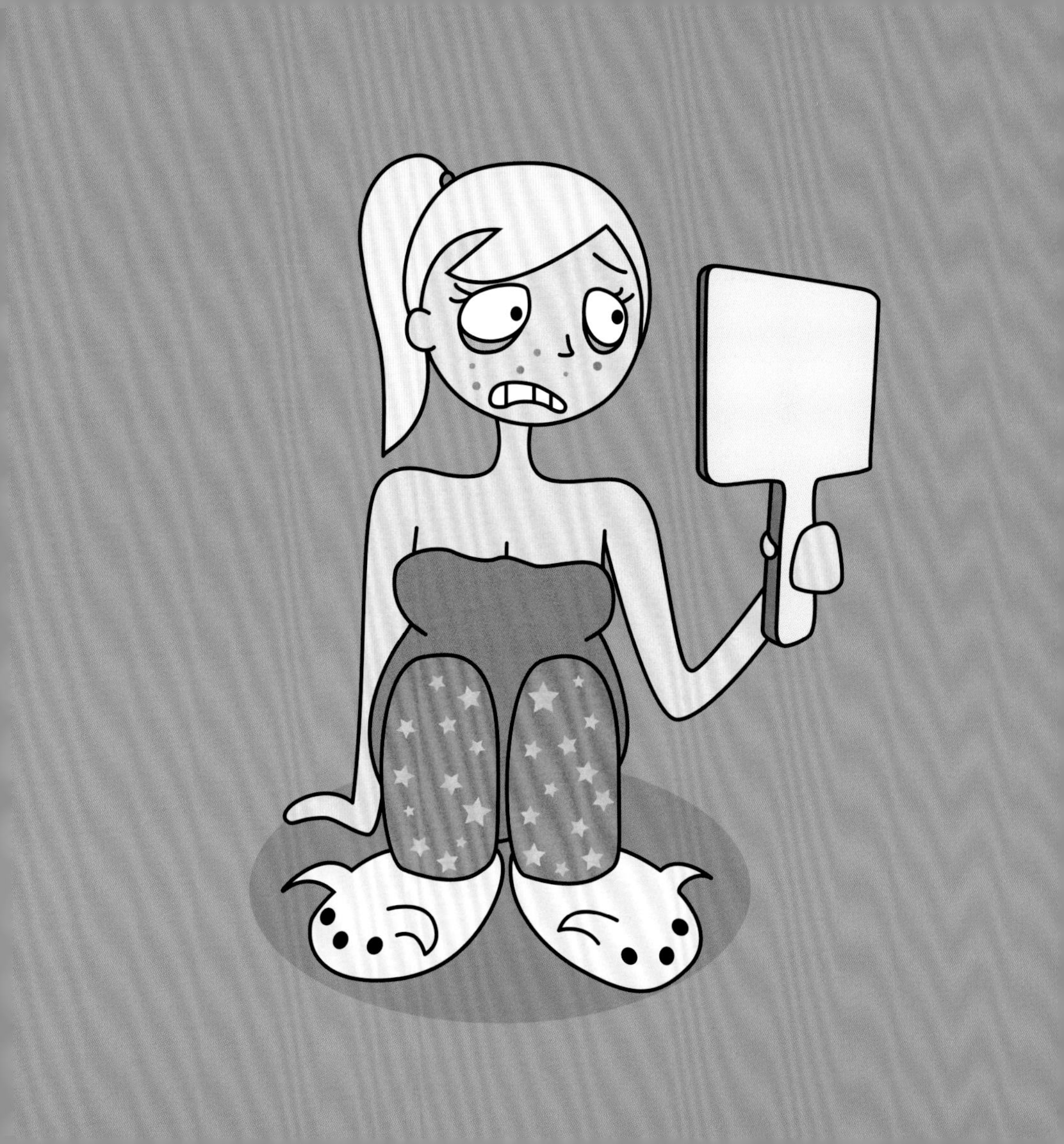

What it's like announcing you're pregnant to your loved ones:

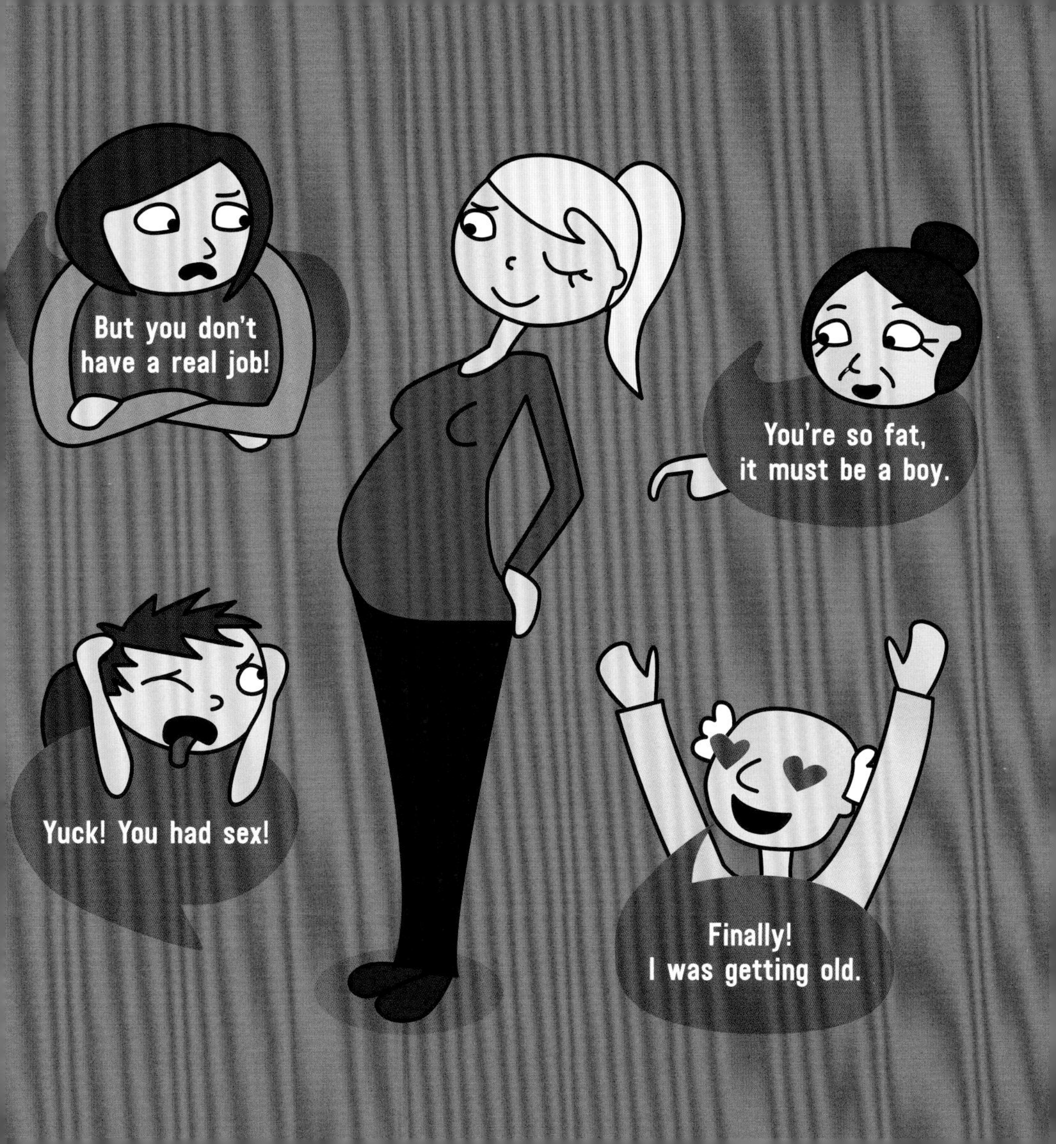
But you don't have a real job!
You're so fat, it must be a boy.
Yuck! You had sex!
Finally! I was getting old.

I'm pretty sure you're just
touching my breakfast there.

See, the baby has your nose.

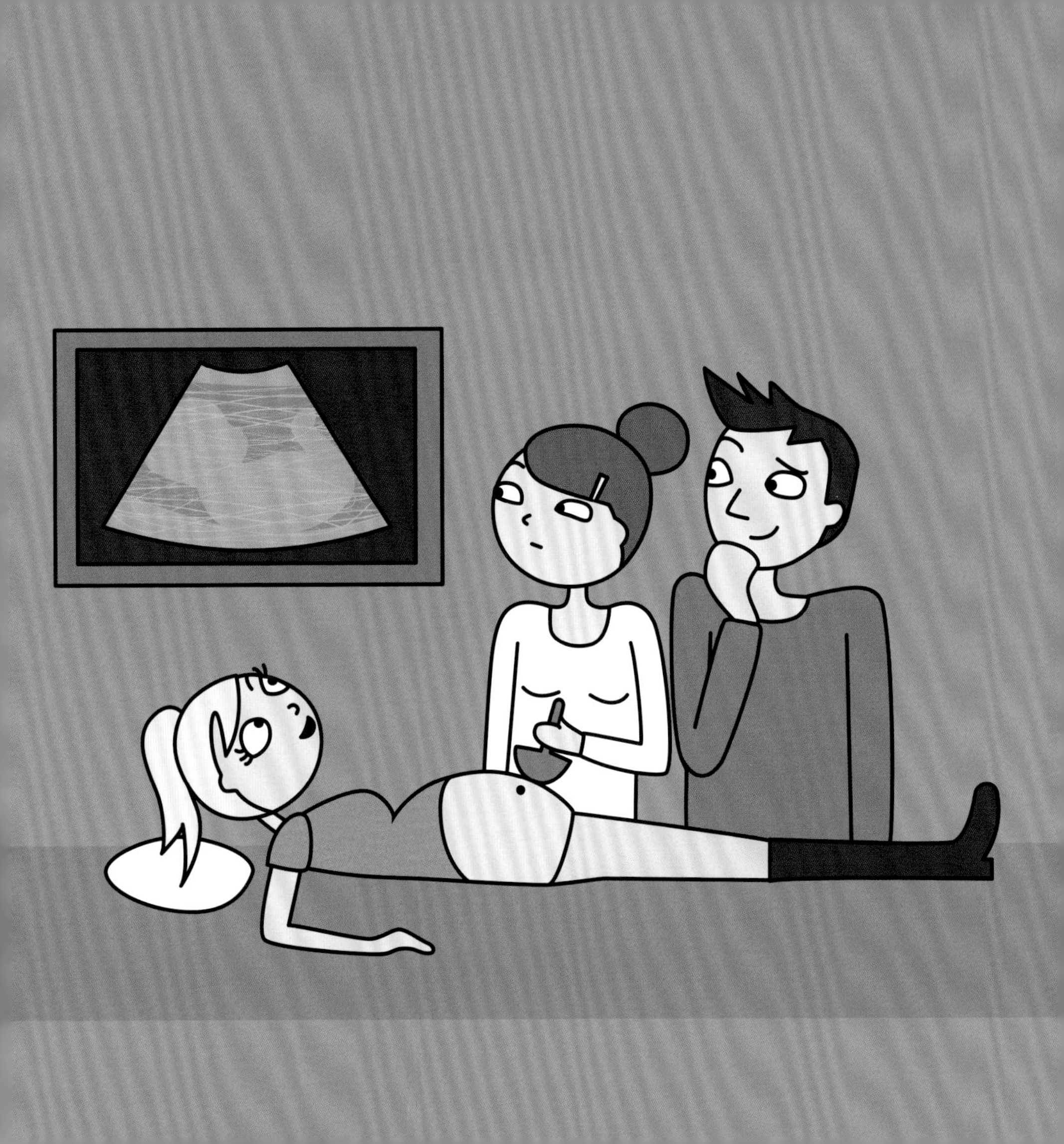

I'm never going back to regular jeans.

Did you know the baby pees inside there?

Just when I need you the most . . .

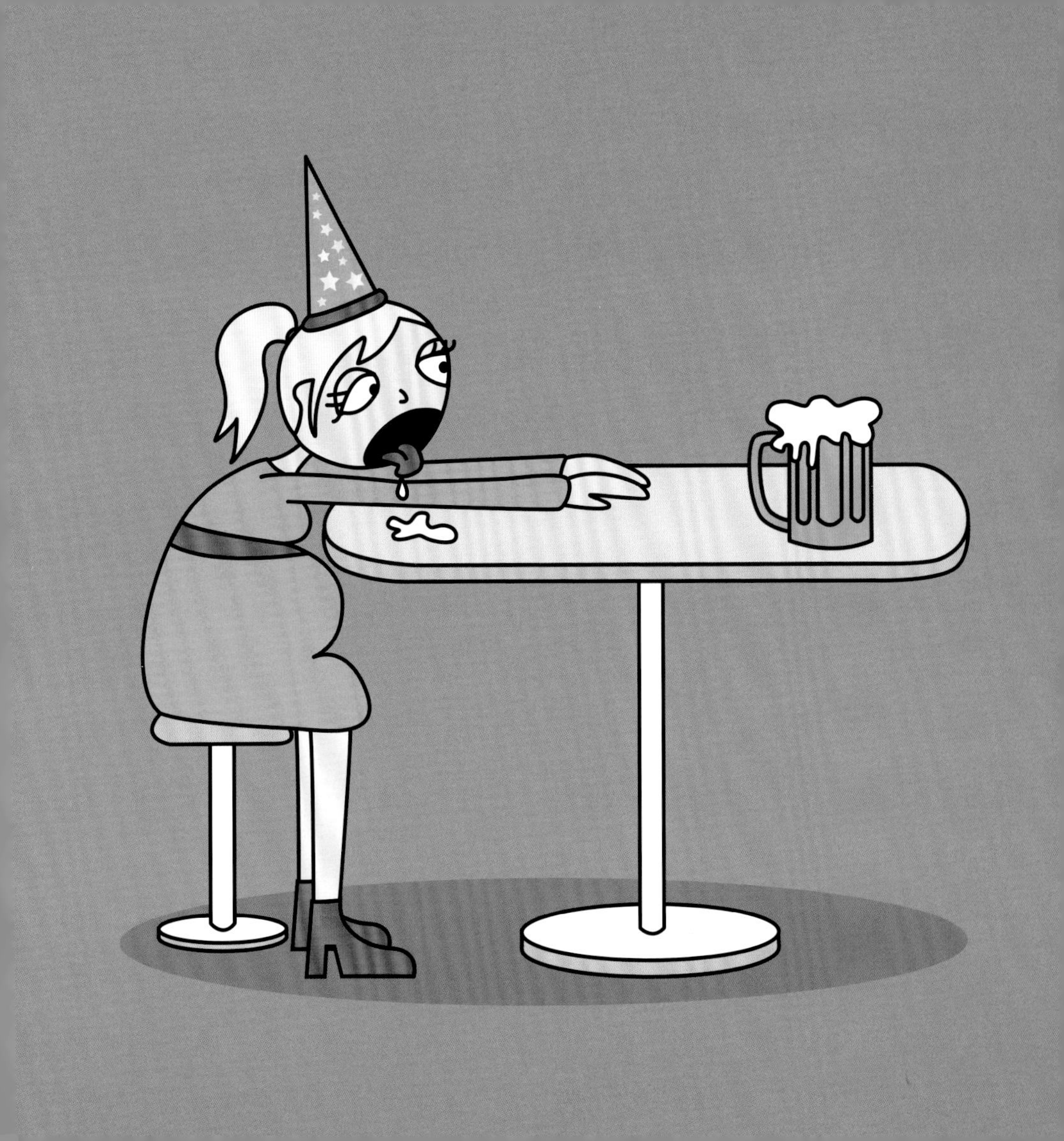

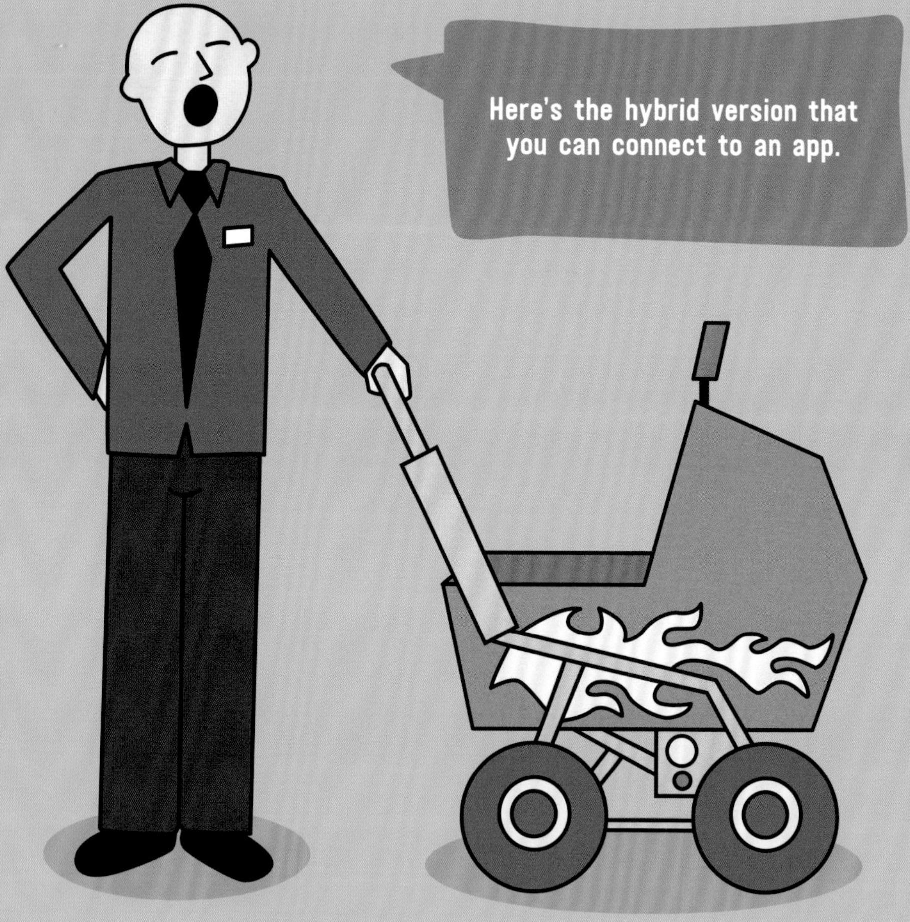
Here's the hybrid version that you can connect to an app.

The baby would love it
if you rubbed my back.

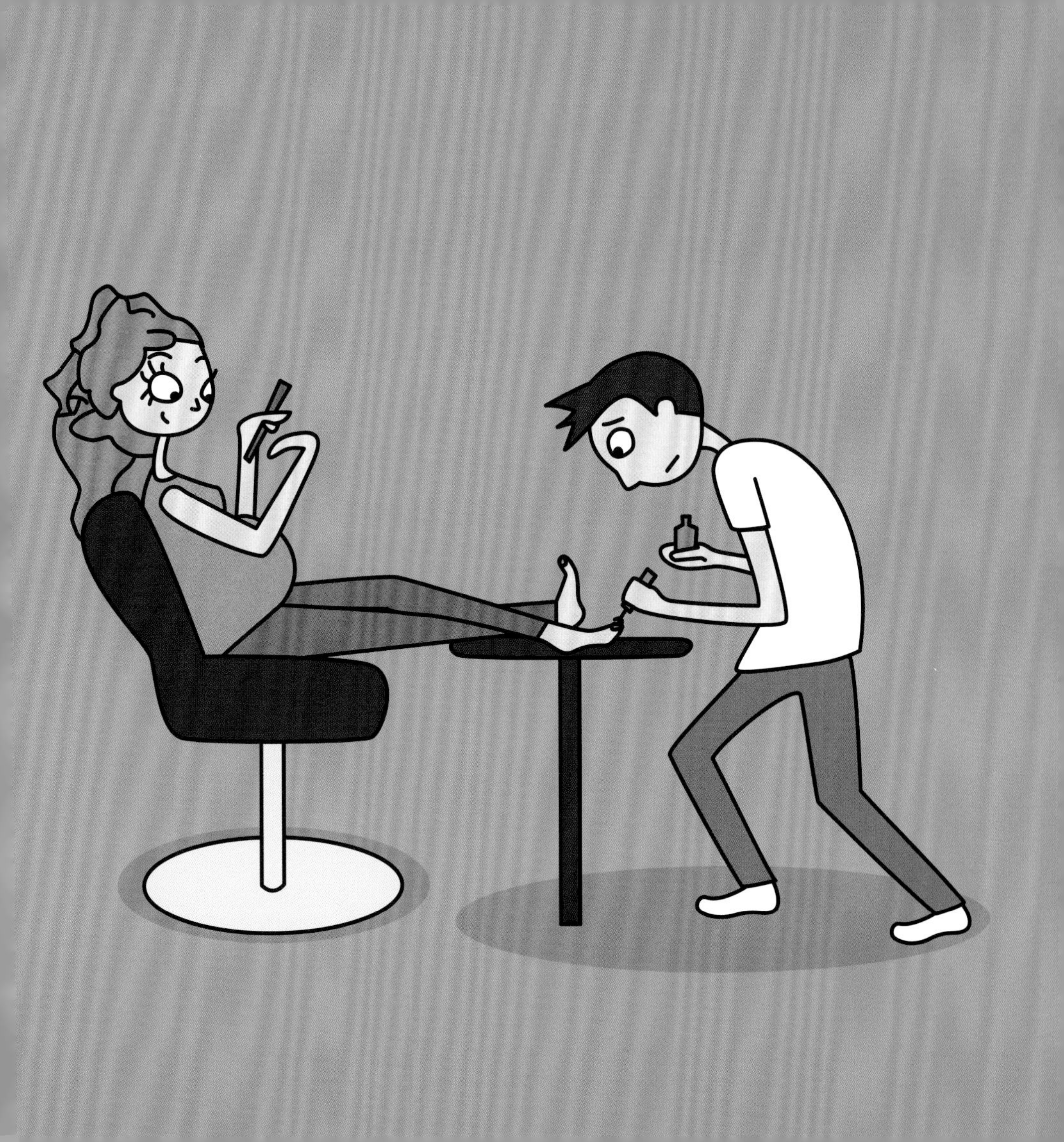

I gave birth to a full-grown man last night.

#PregnancyHormoneNightmare

One chocolate for me,
and one for the baby.

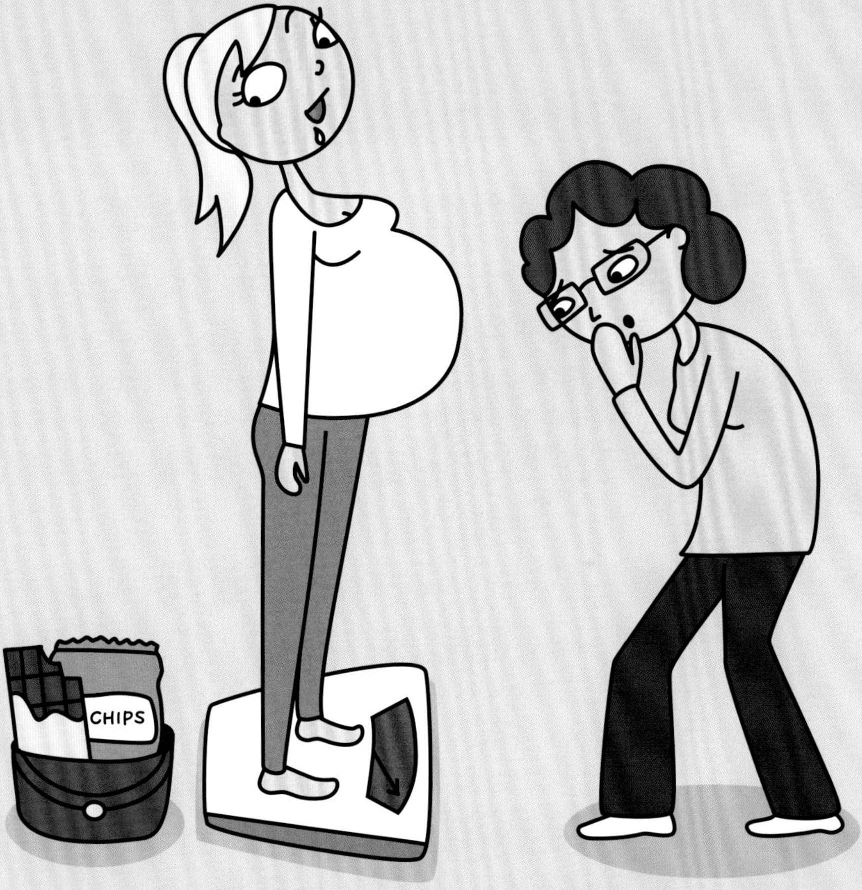
CHIPS

Where can I find ice cream
with pickles at 2 A.M.?

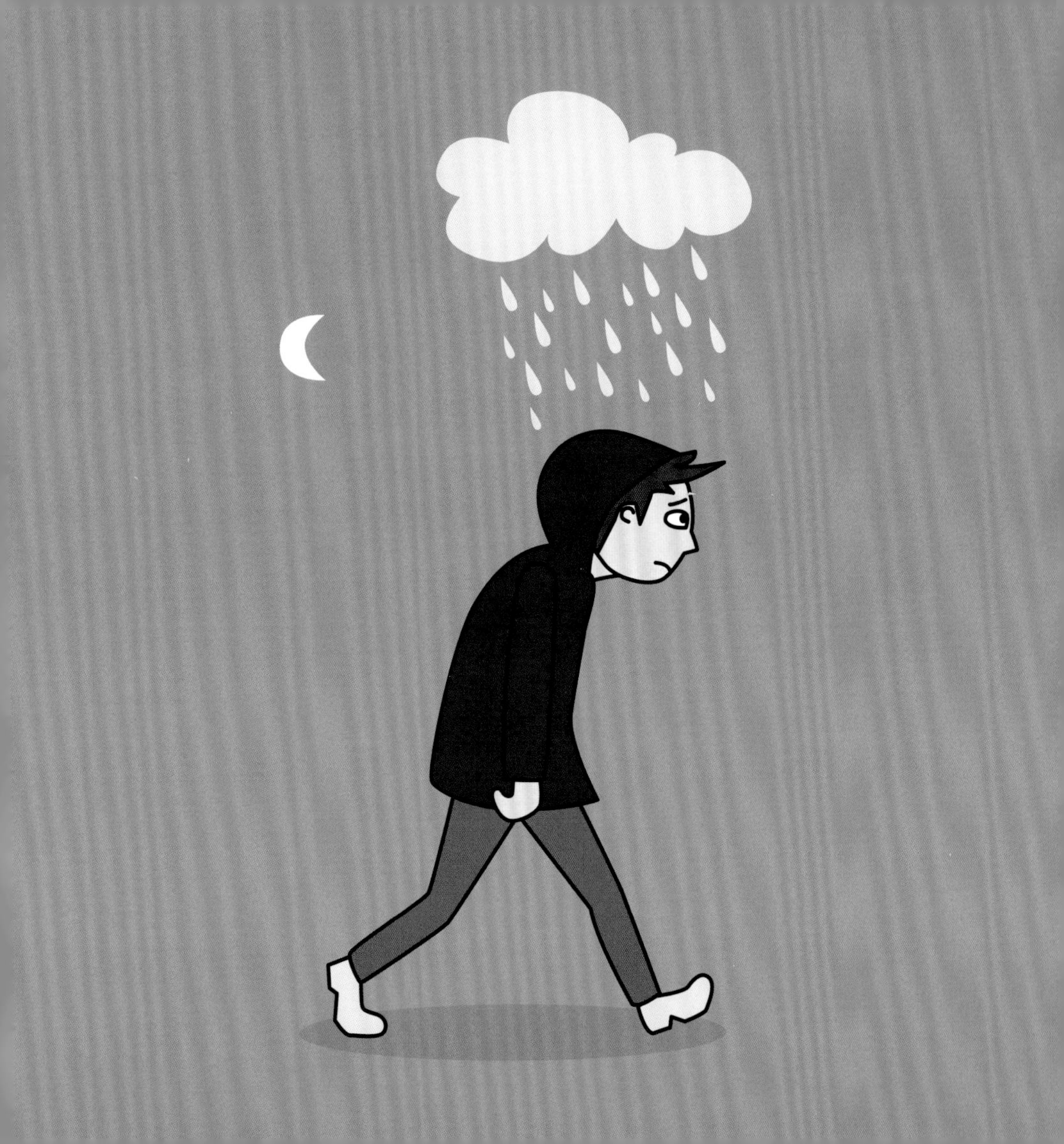

Whoops! Blame the baby.

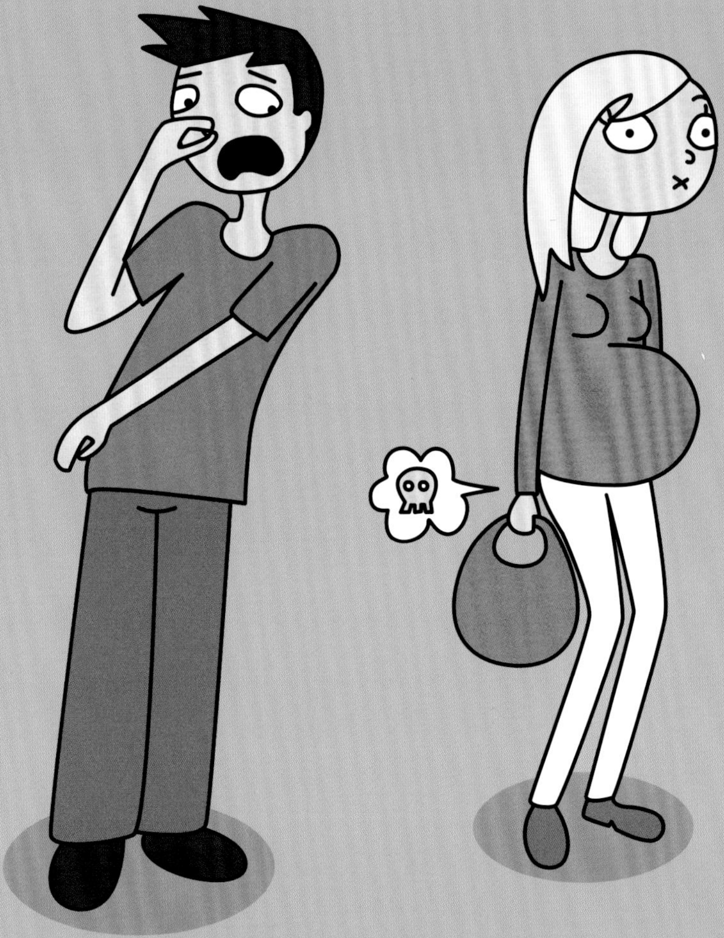

Fzzzz

Fzzzz

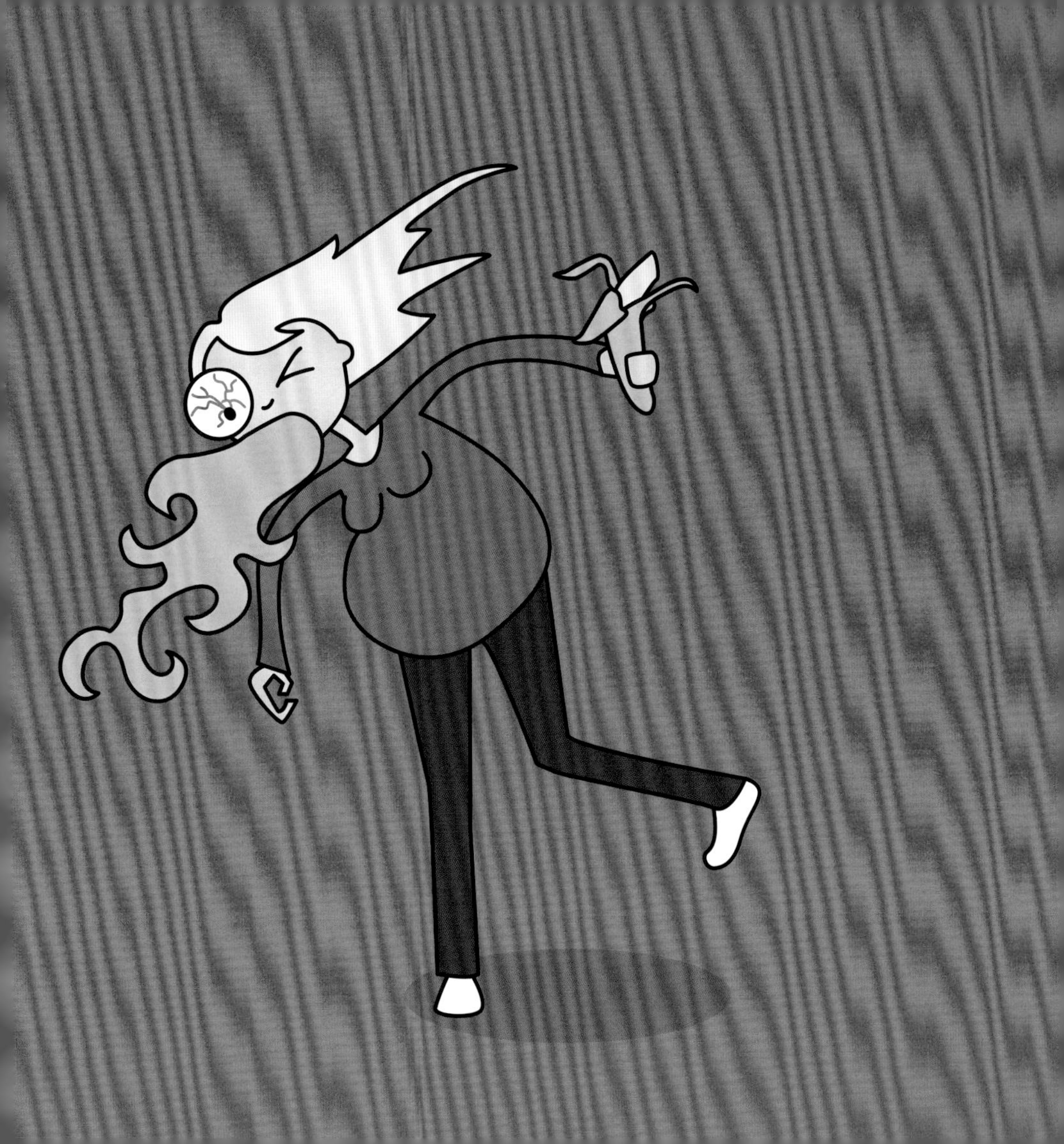

I need a parking space
just for my belly.

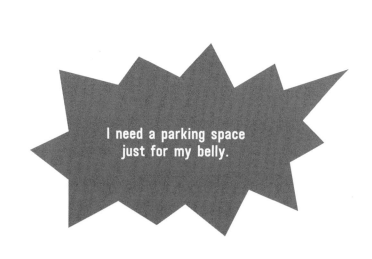

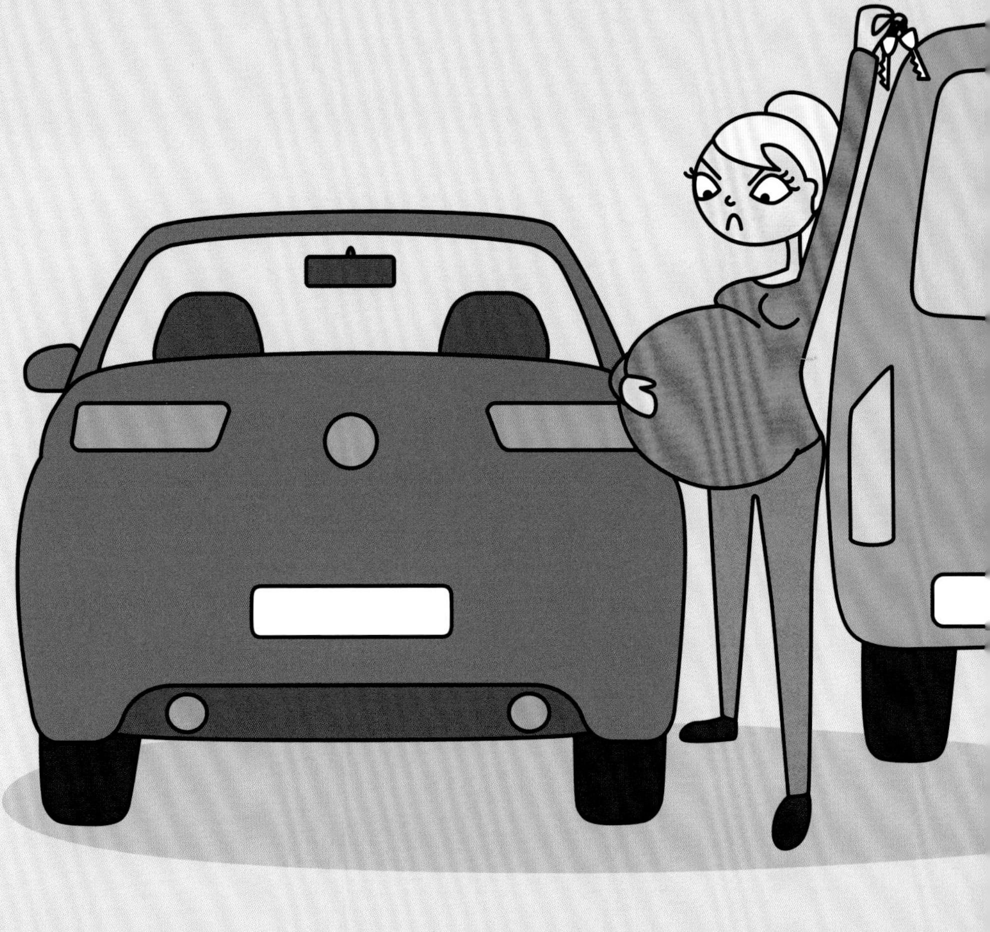

If I remove these,
will the baby get cold?

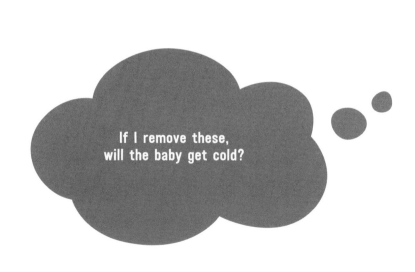

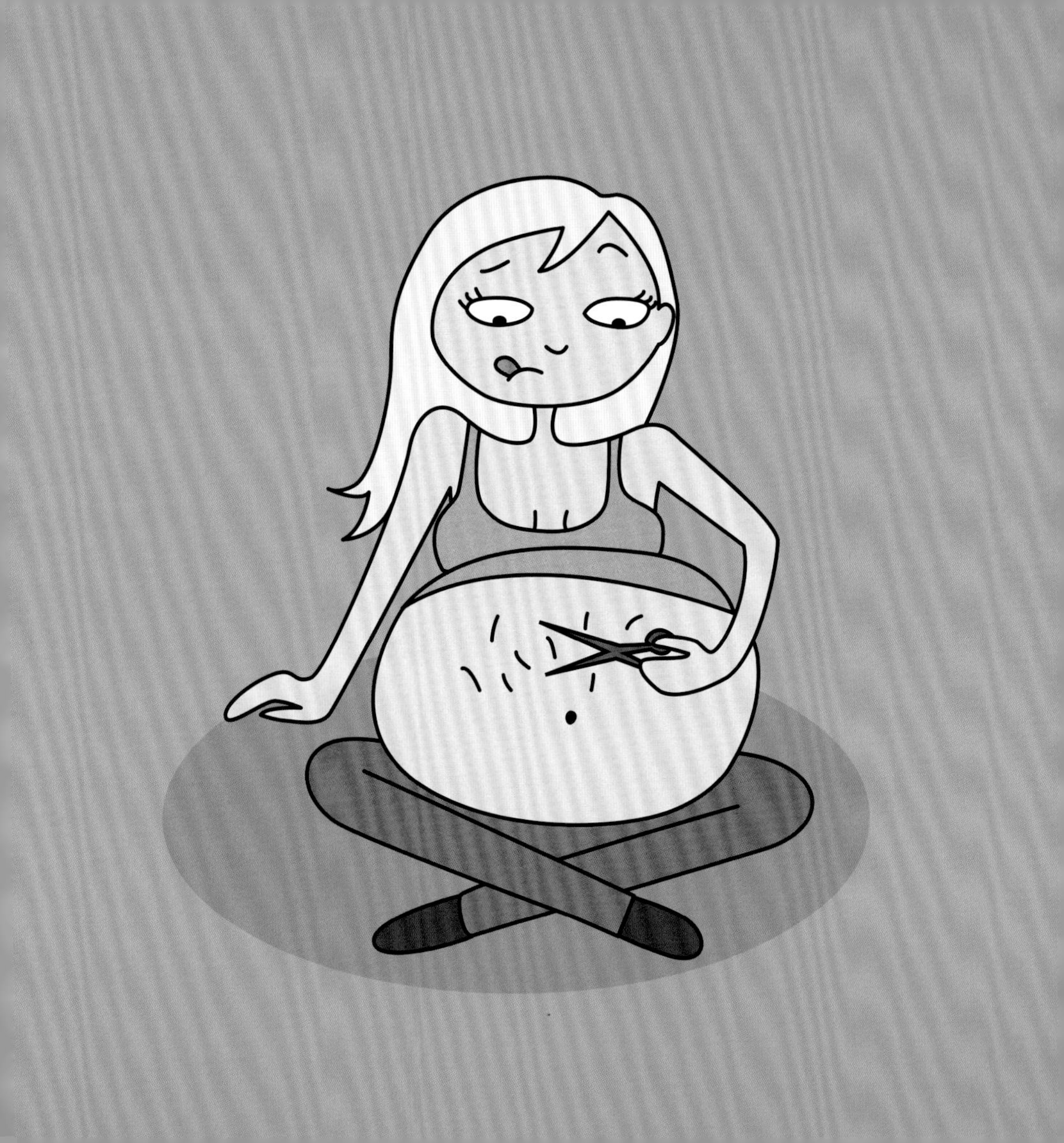

Can't . . . stop . . . scratching!

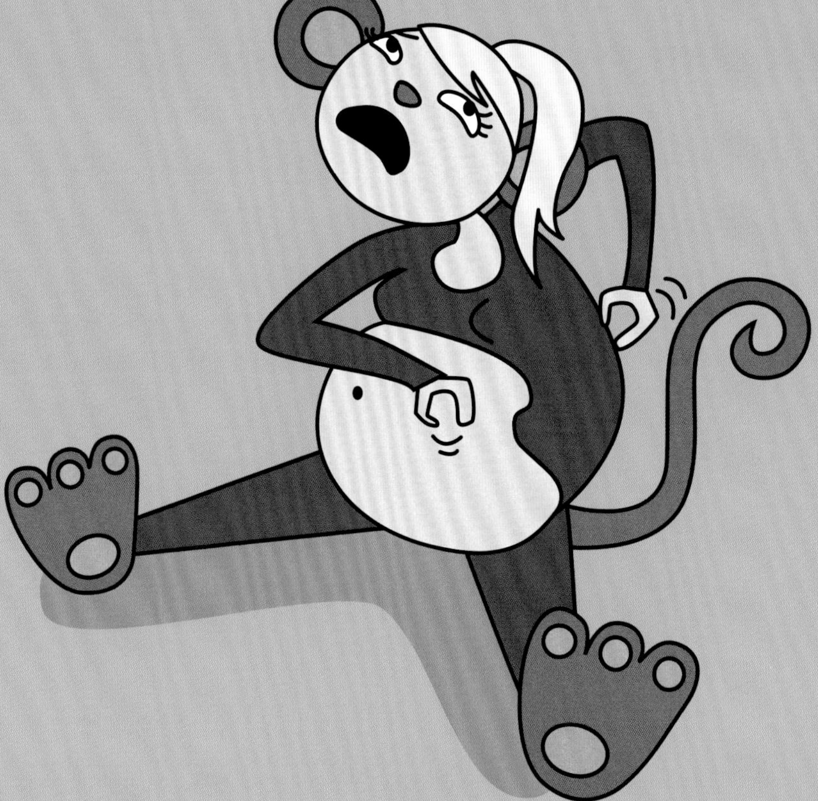

Nope! The baby will not be named
Lisa, or Tiffany, or Chris . . .

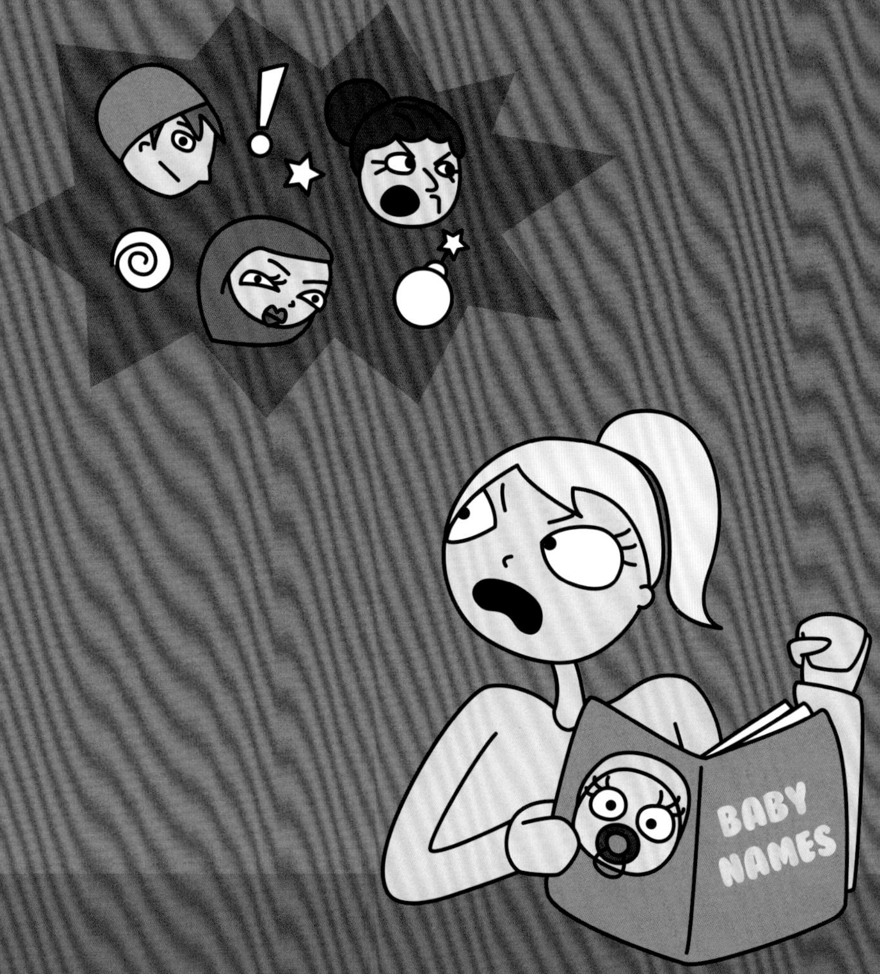
BABY
NAMES

It's just so beautiful!

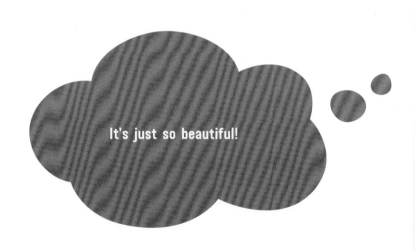

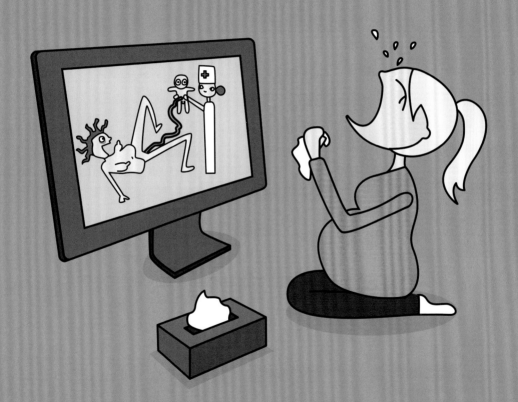

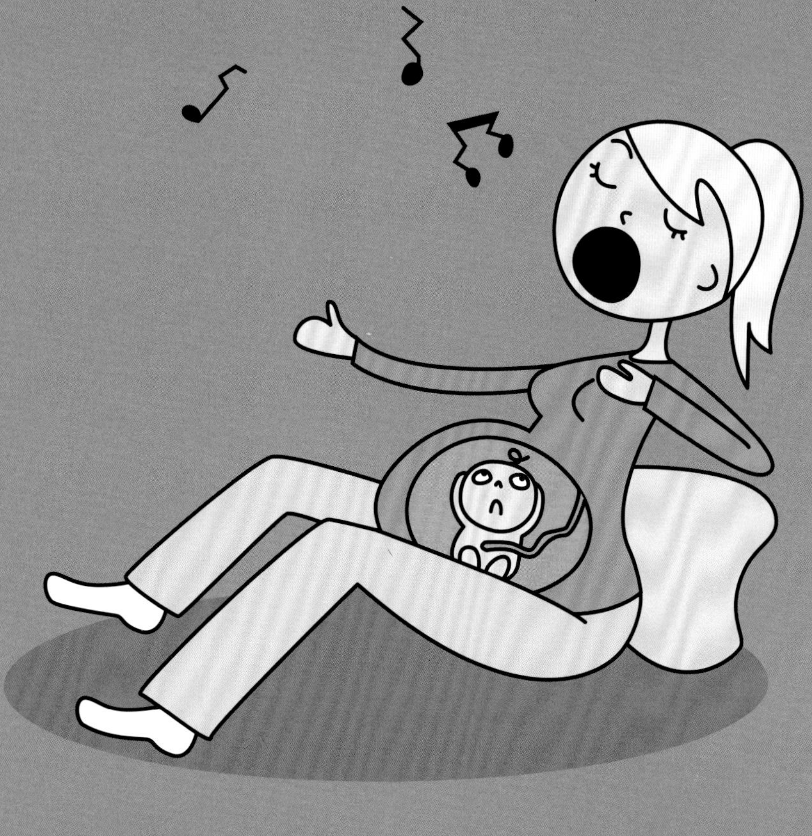

Yoga! Not karate!

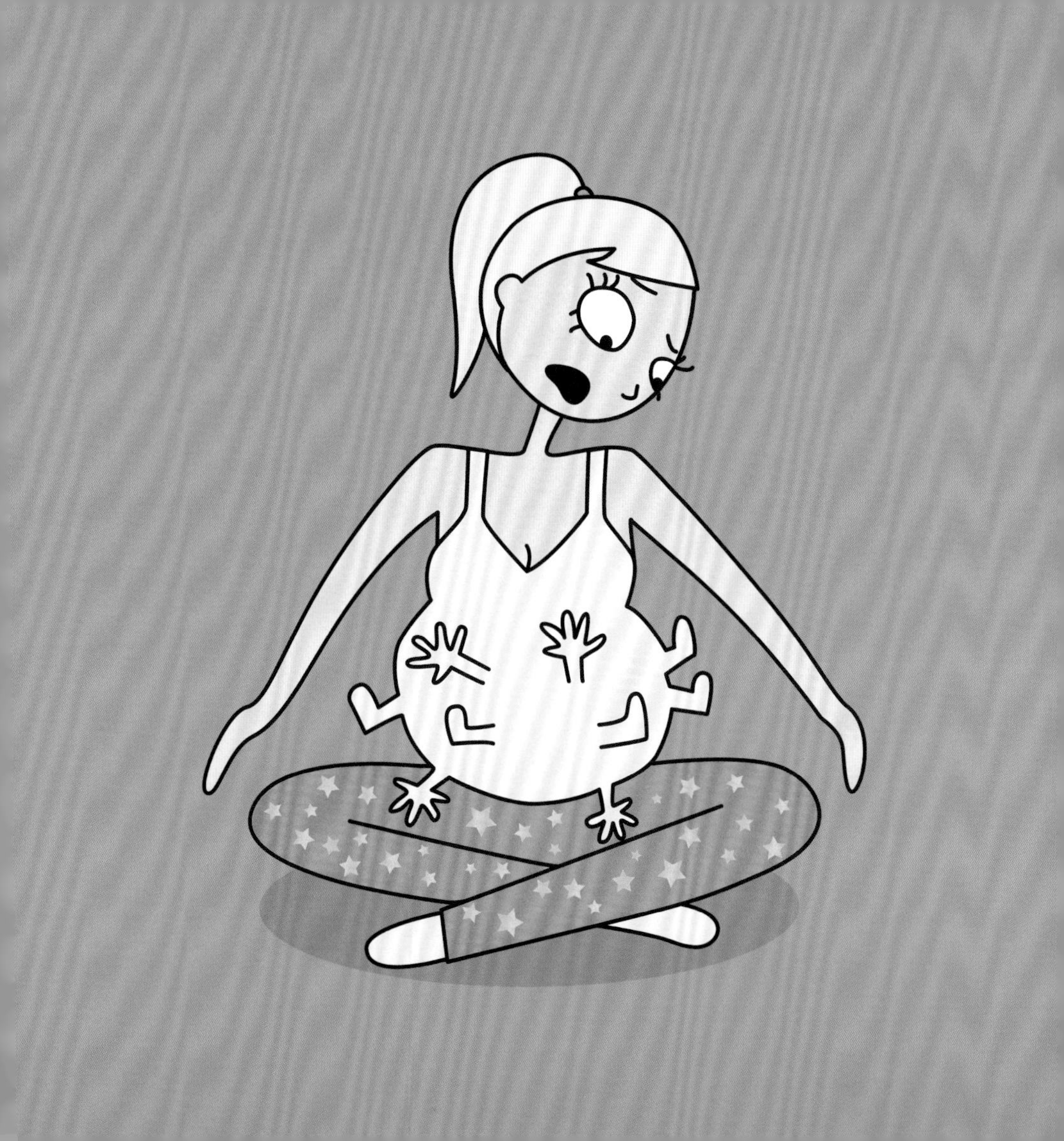

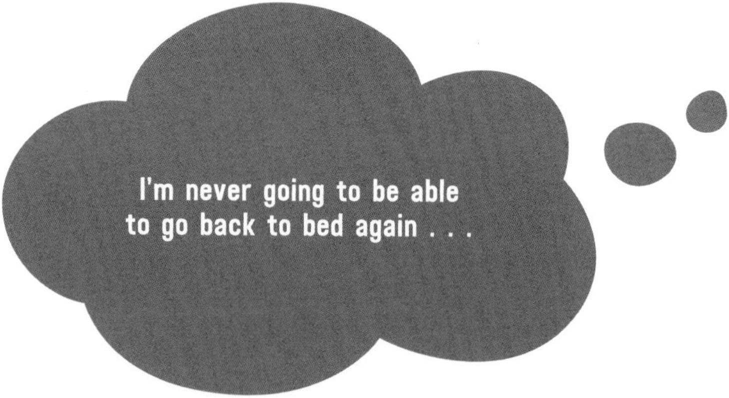
I'm never going to be able
to go back to bed again . . .

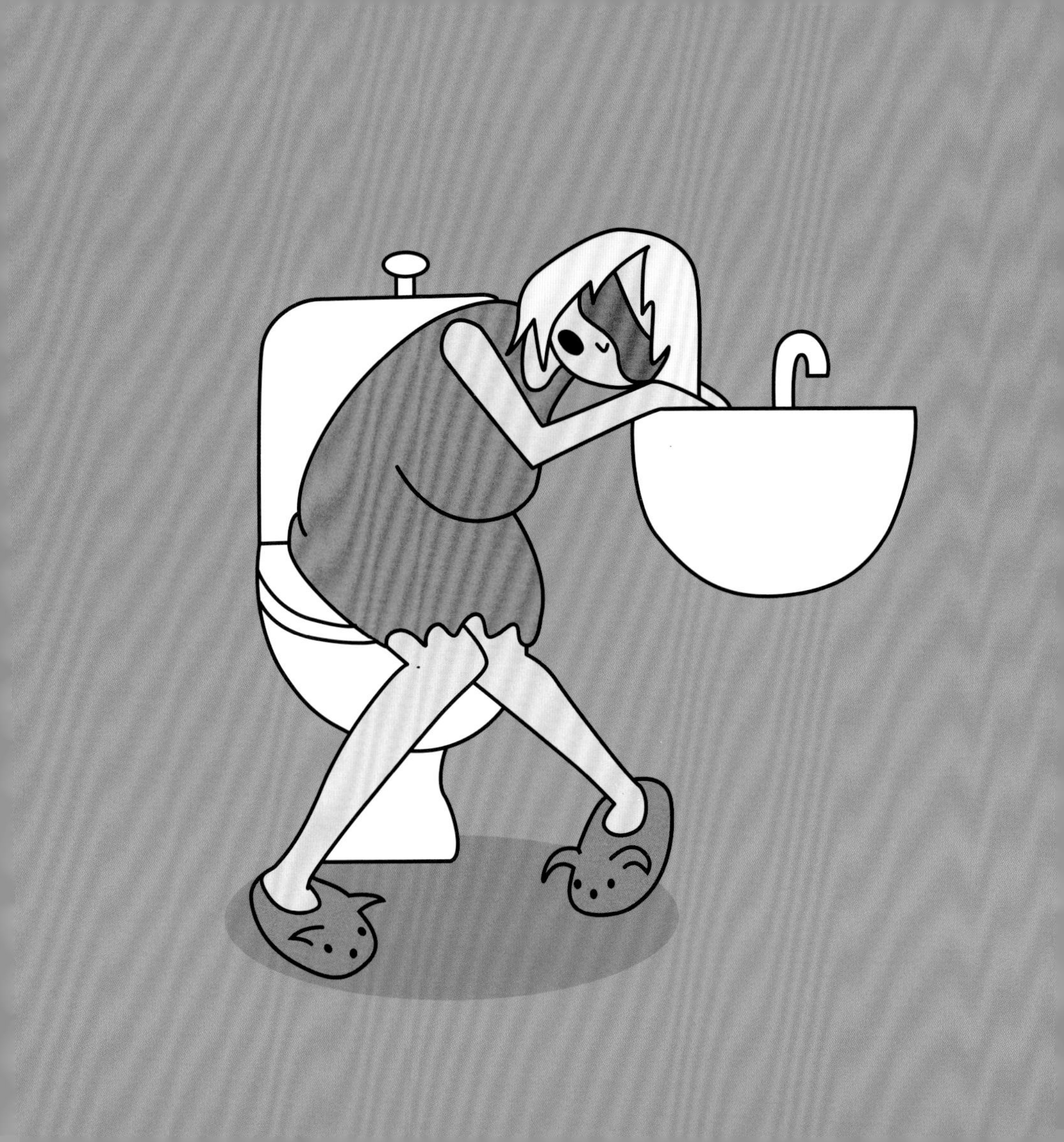

I think we need a bigger car . . .

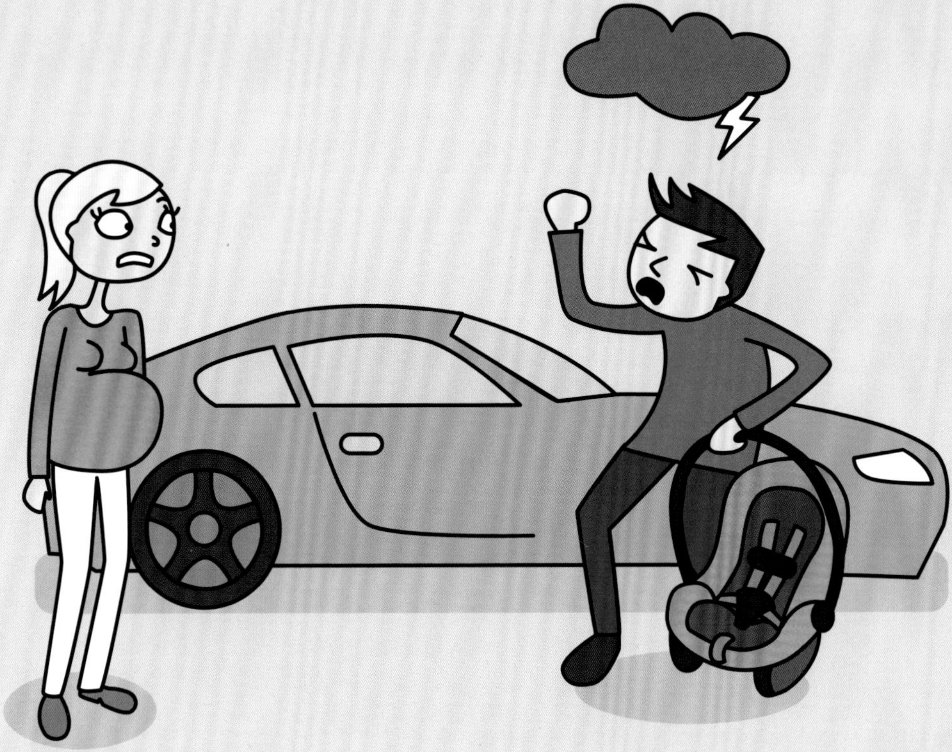

Work harder!
We have to impress the baby!

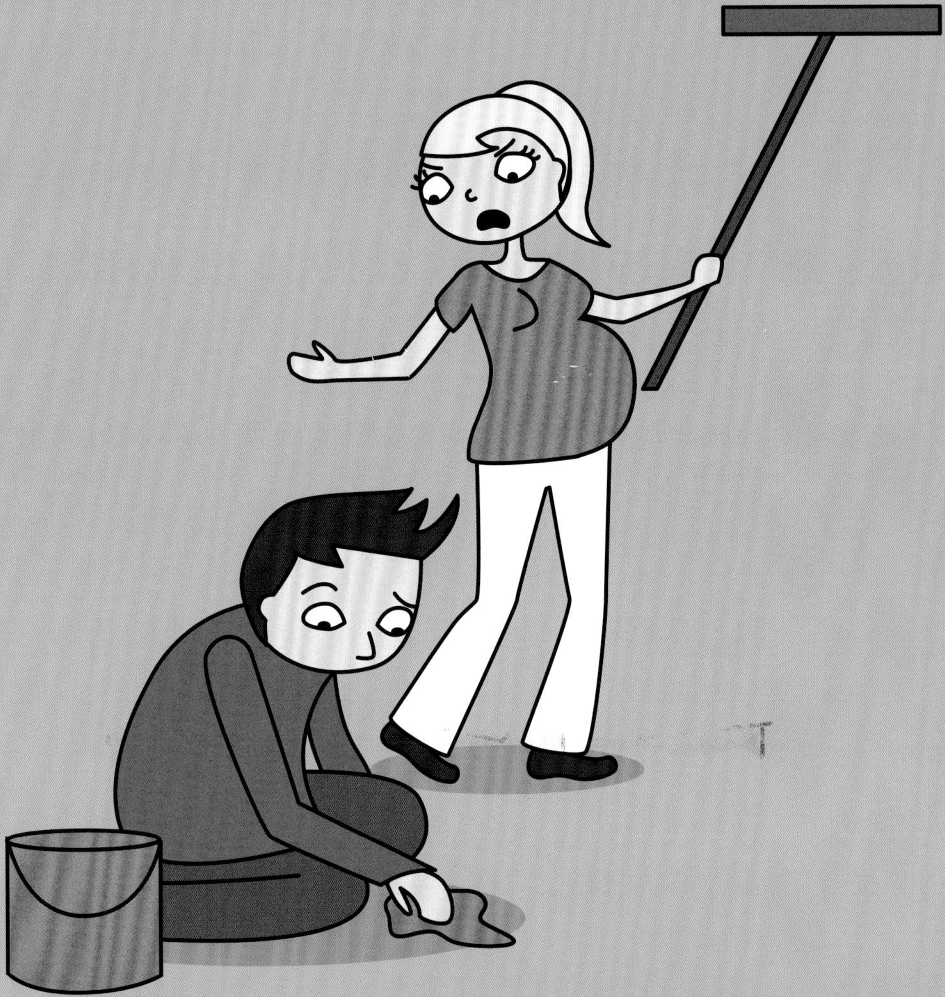

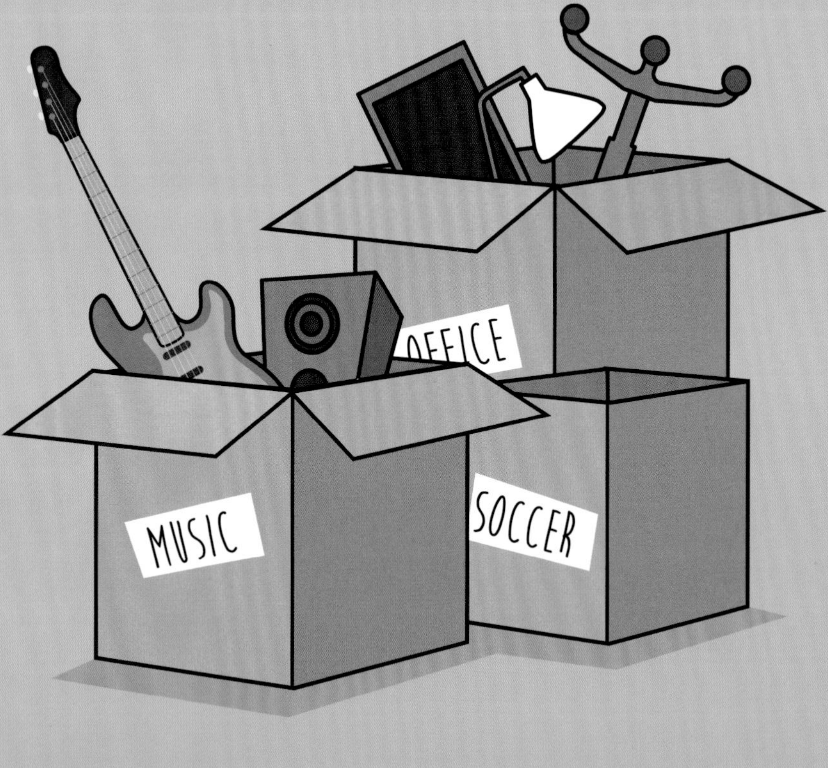
OFFICE
MUSIC
SOCCER

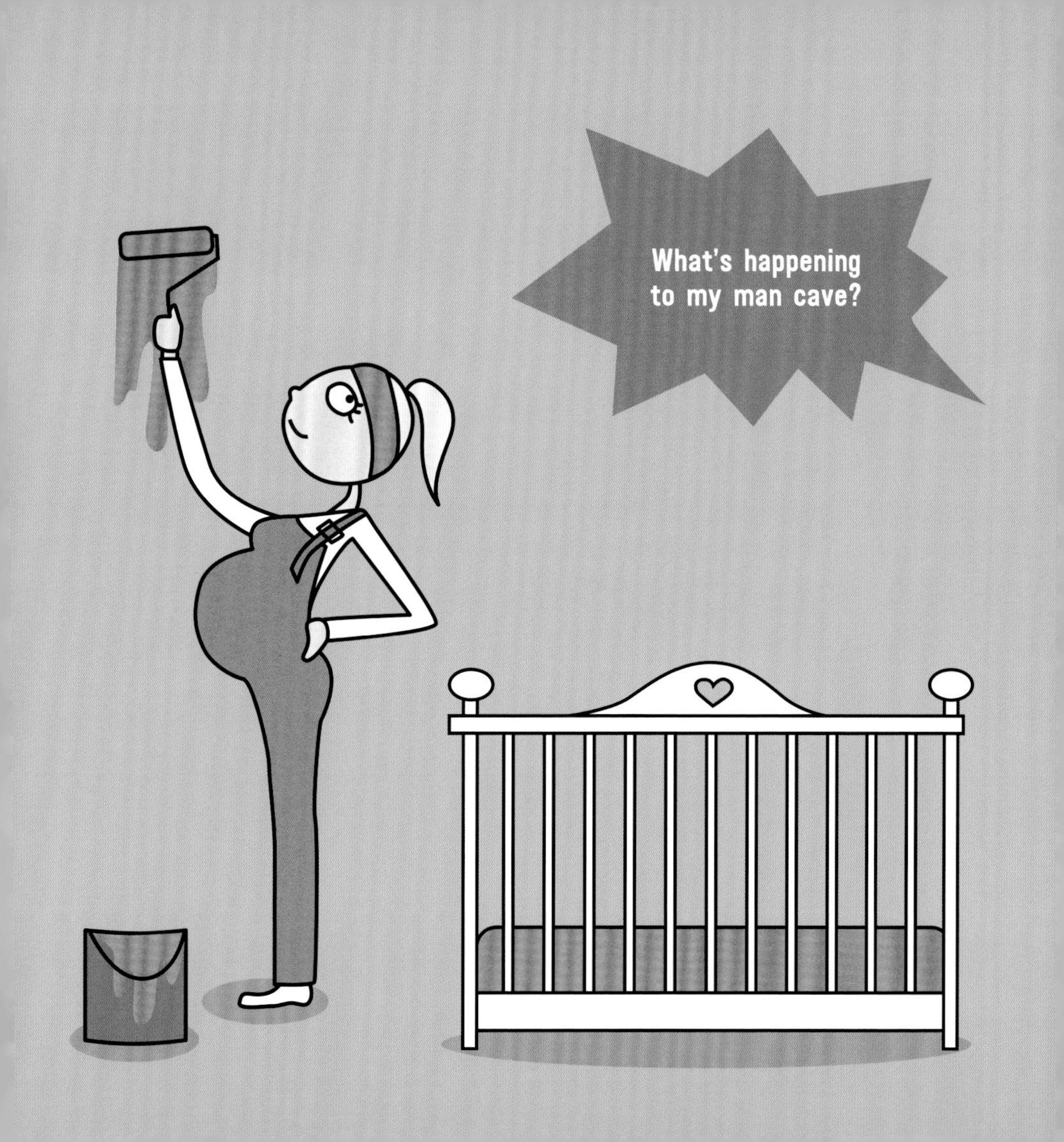
What's happening to my man cave?

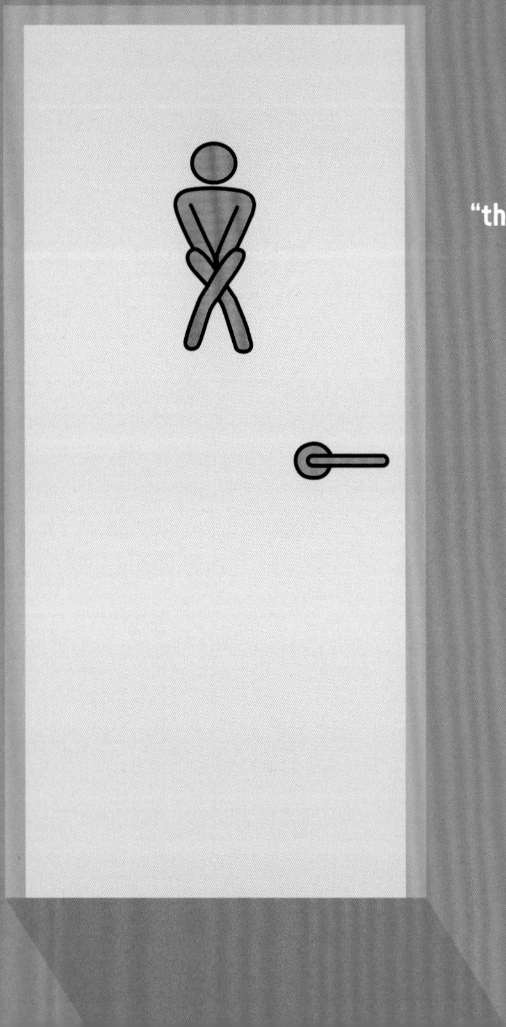

I call this
"the third-trimester workout."

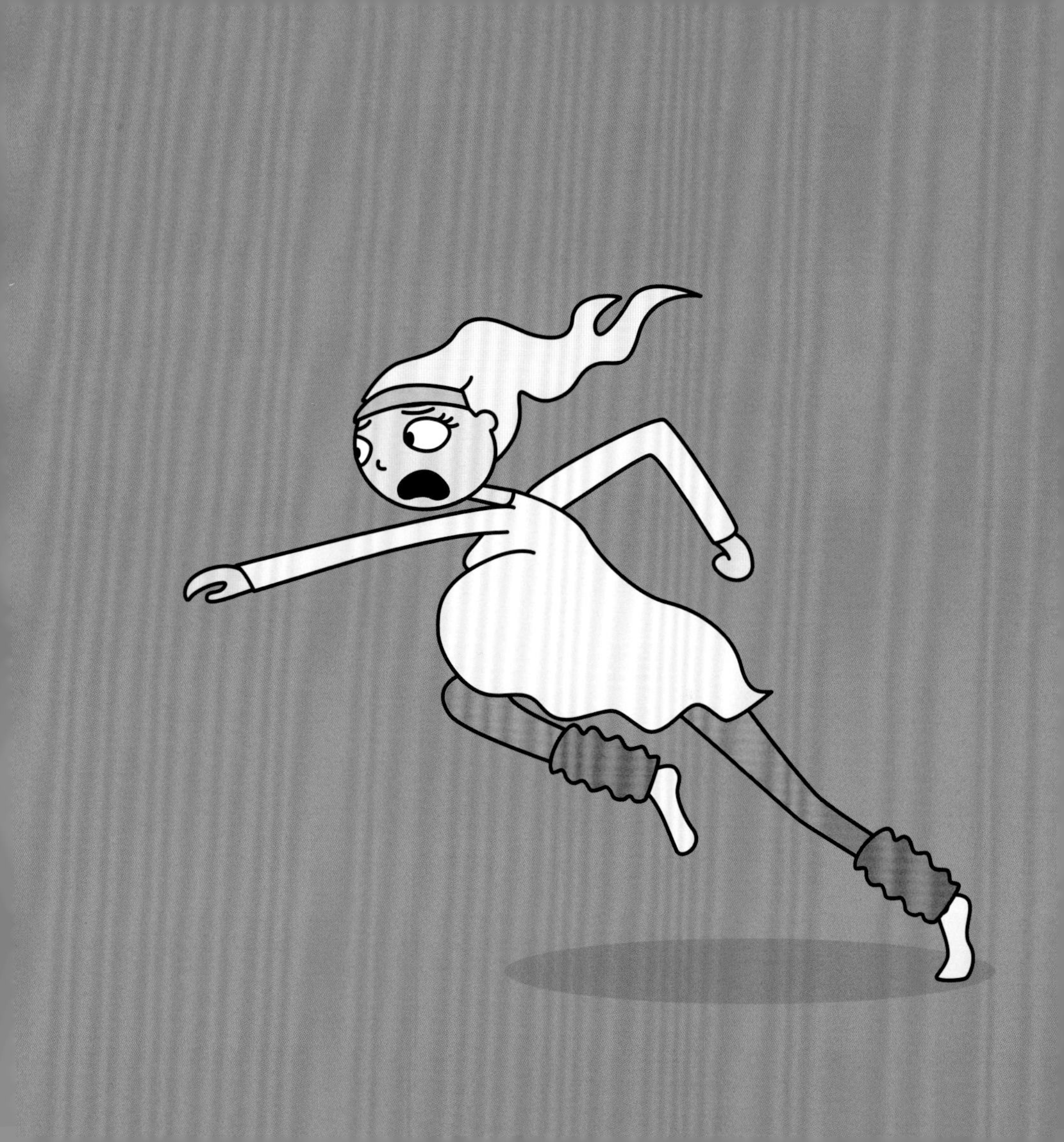

At least I have a built-in table.

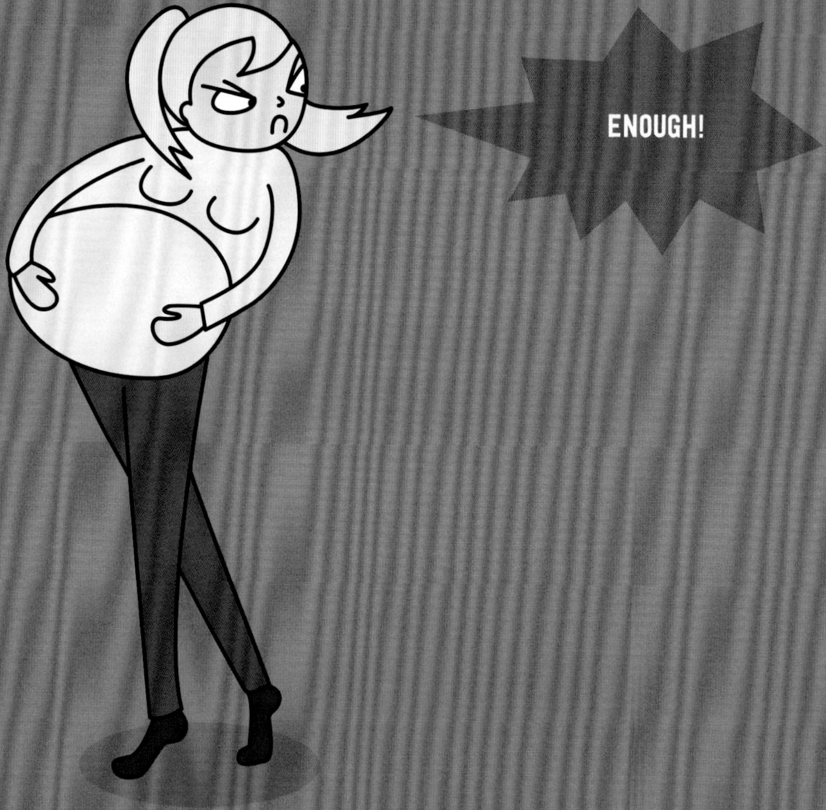
ENOUGH!

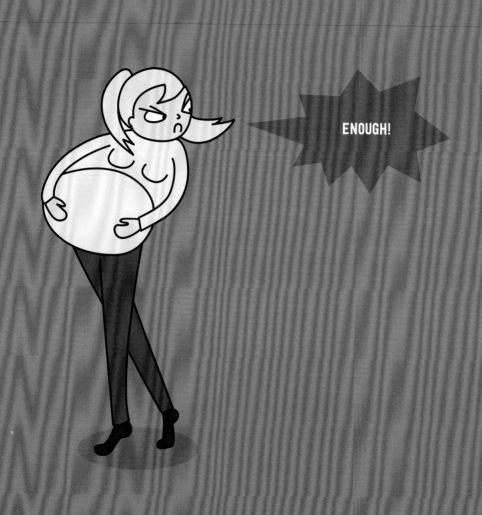

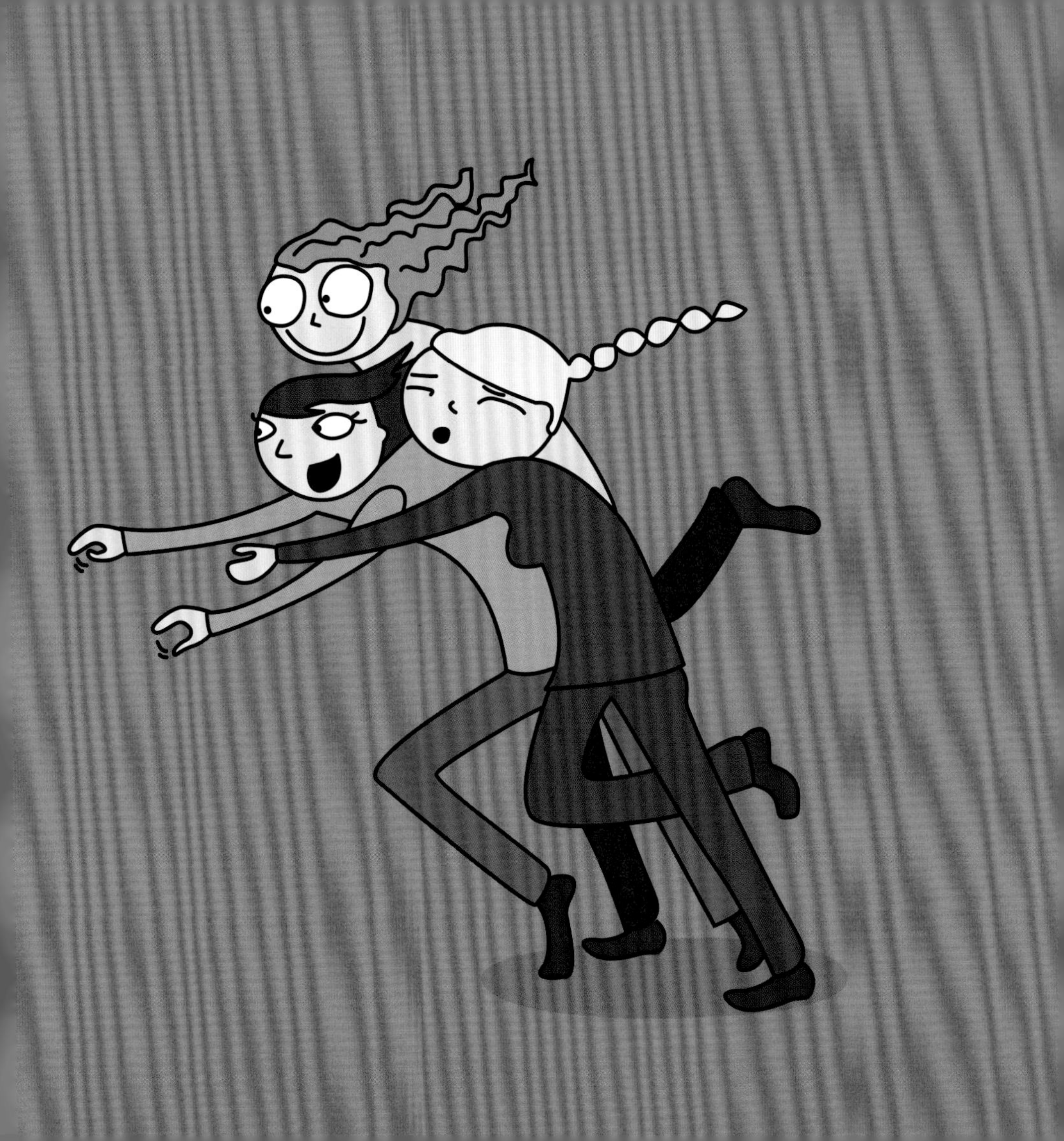

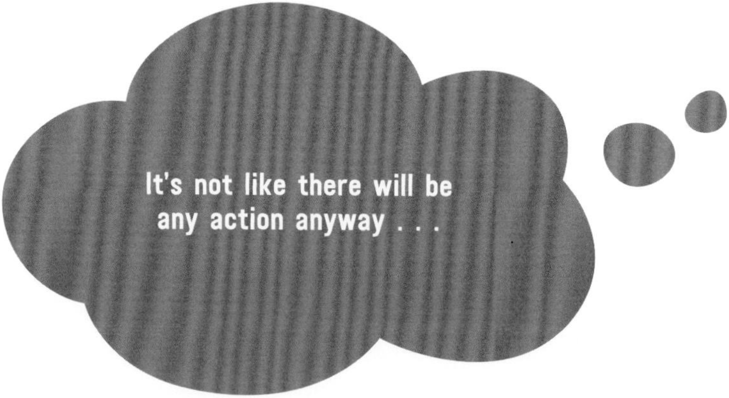
It's not like there will be any action anyway . . .

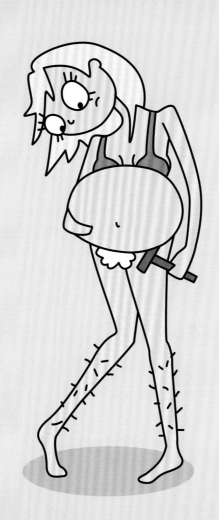

I poked the baby!!!

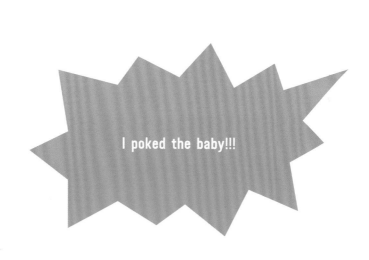

Tell me more about how you don't think pregnancy is a disease.

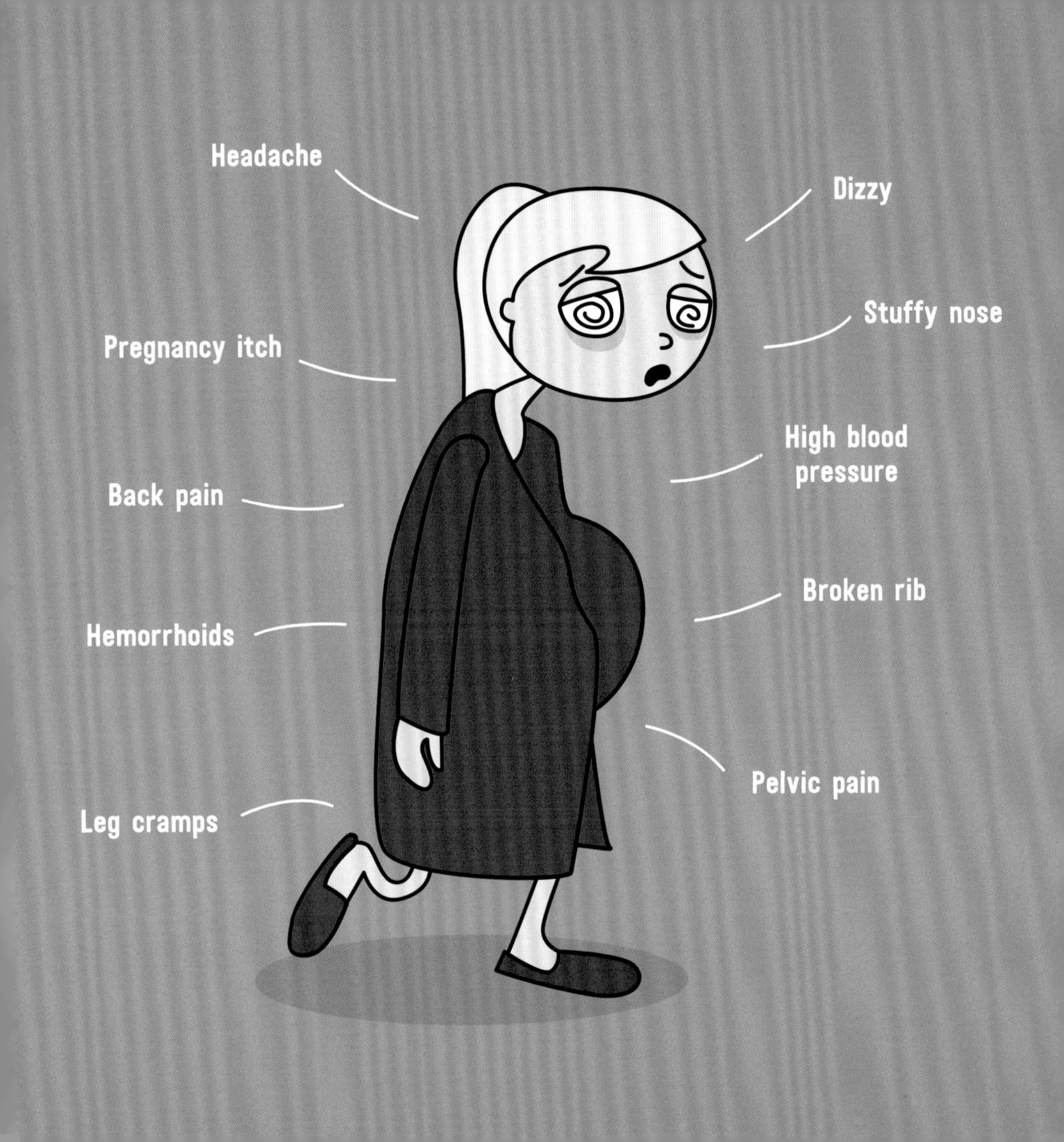
Headache
Dizzy
Stuffy nose
Pregnancy itch
High blood pressure
Back pain
Broken rib
Hemorrhoids
Pelvic pain
Leg cramps

A brand-new white designer couch for our clean new baby.

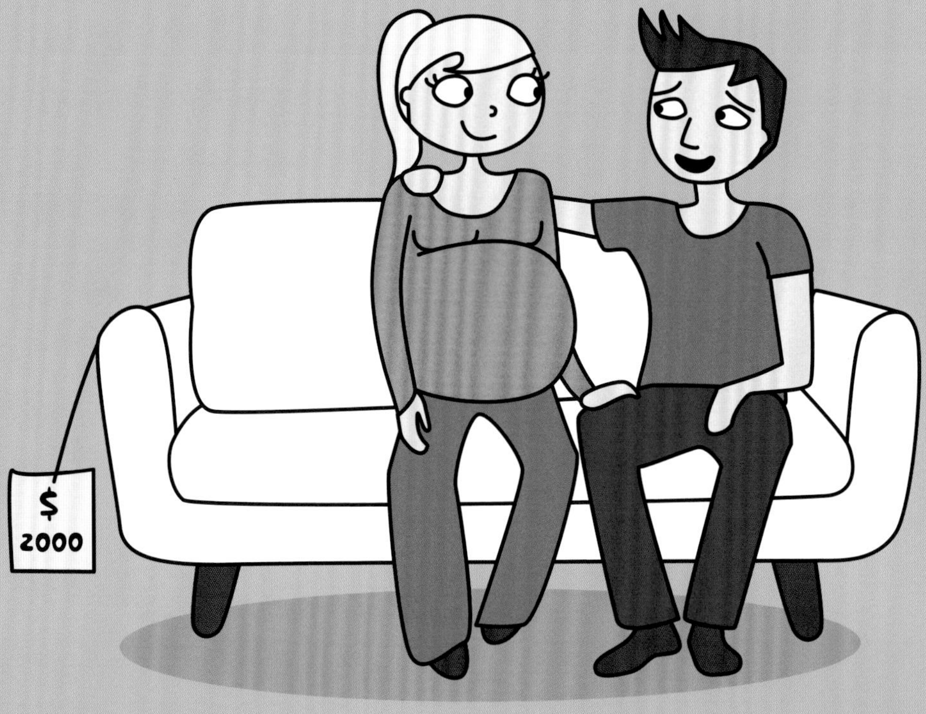
$
2000

The head is now attached . . .

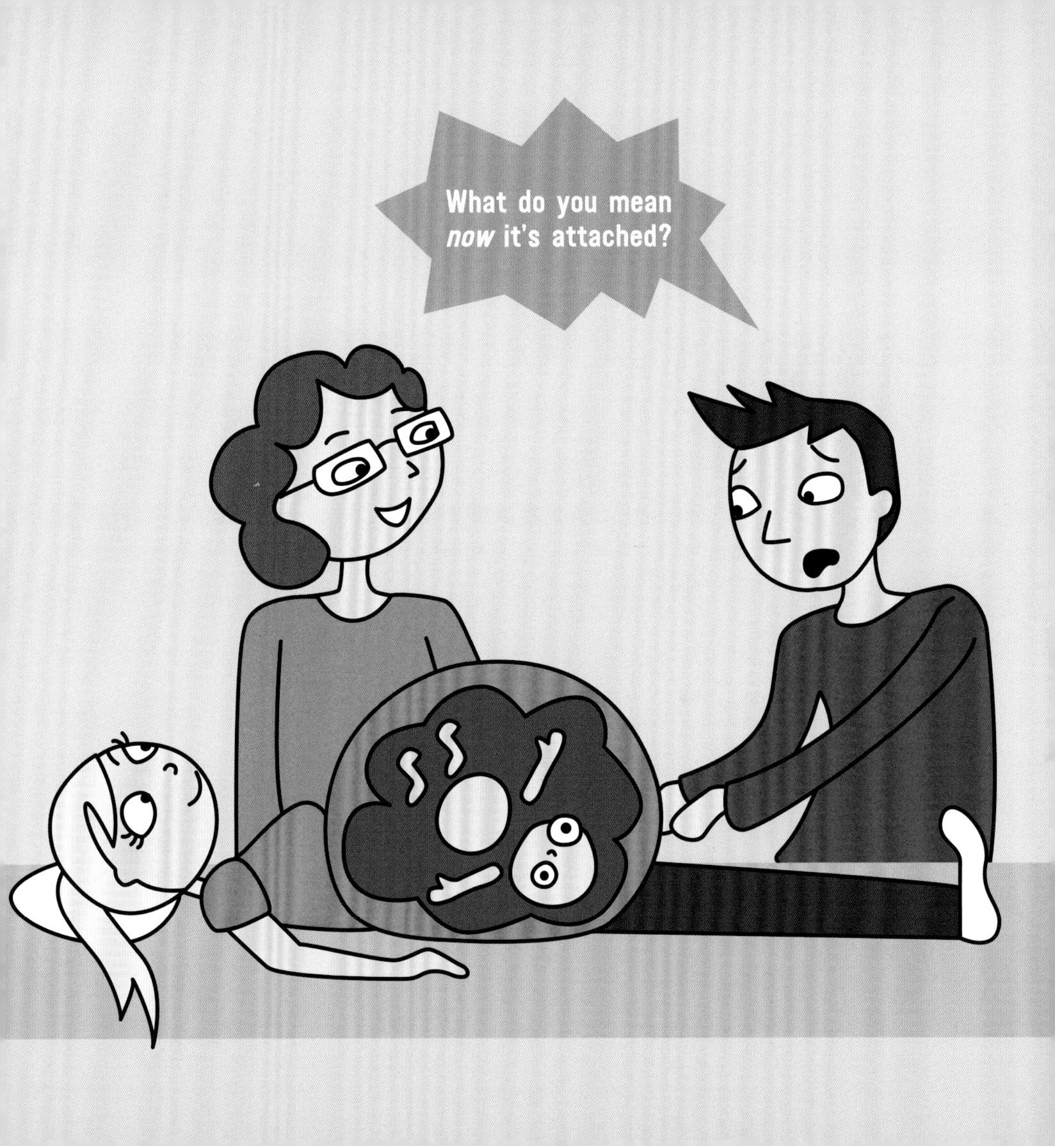
What do you mean *now* it's attached?

It's hard to be chic when you look like a water balloon.

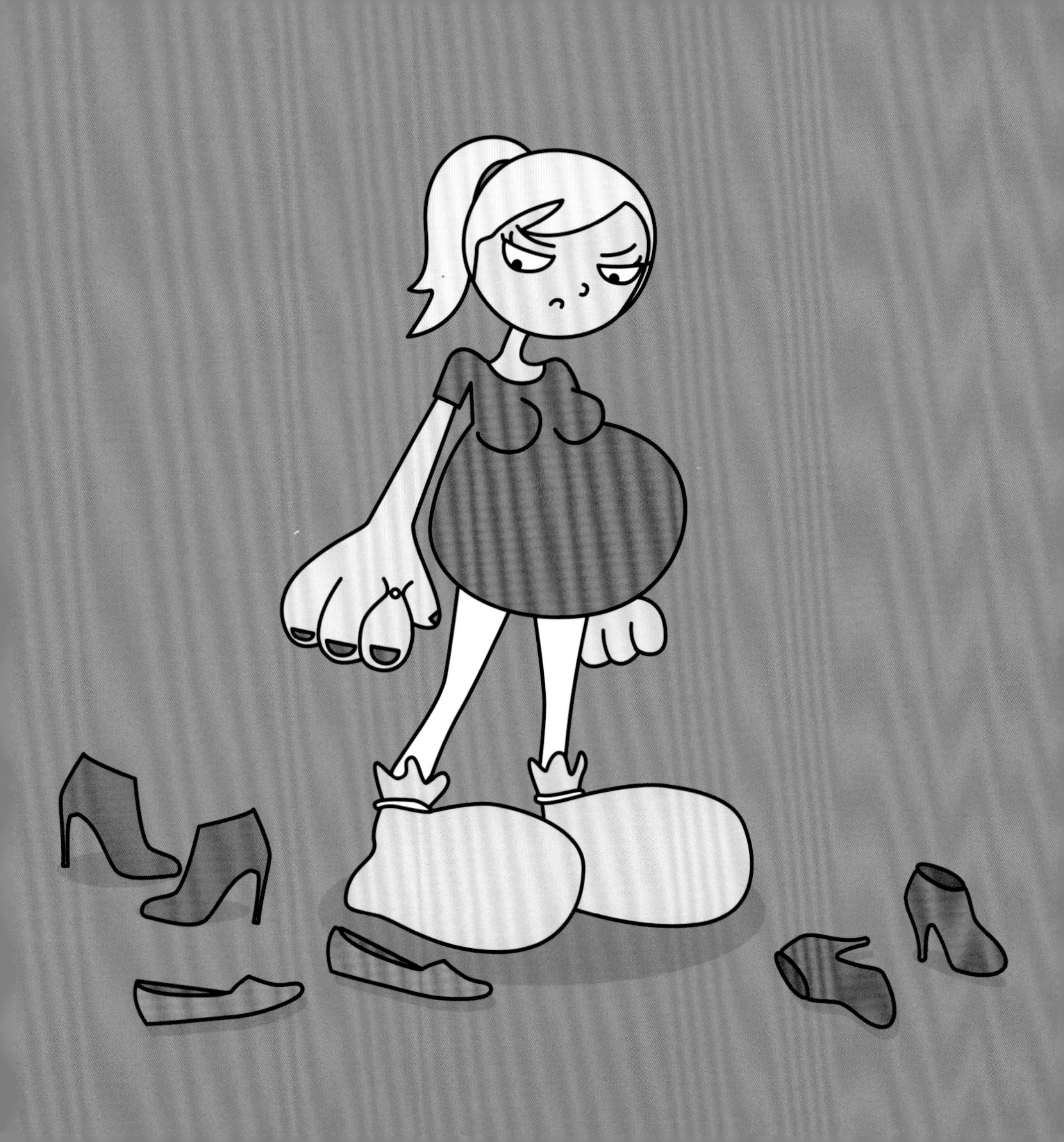

Comments you don't need to hear:

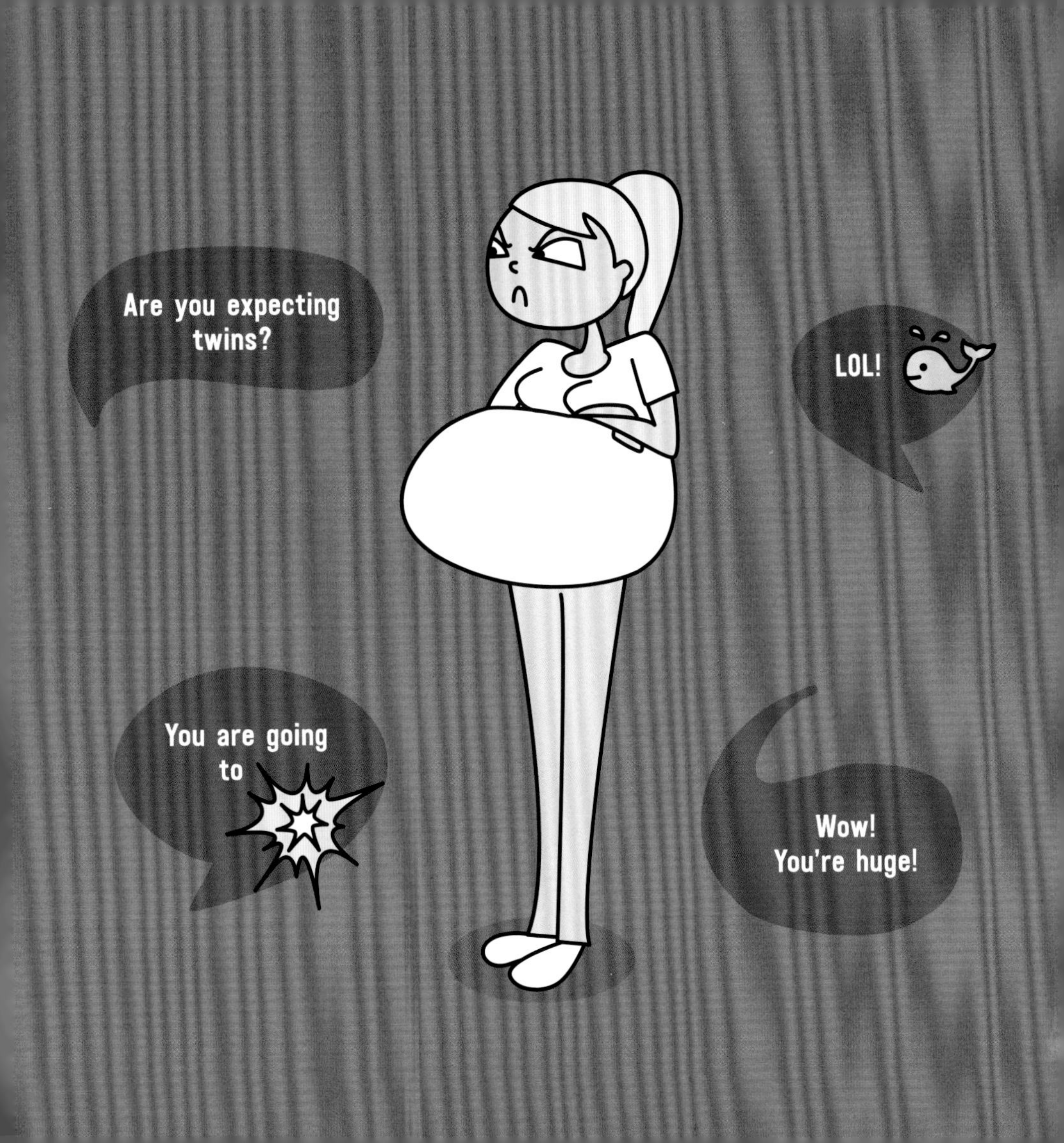
Are you expecting twins?
LOL!
You are going to
Wow! You're huge!

Don't mess with a tired pregnant lady . . .

Time to get some slip-ons.

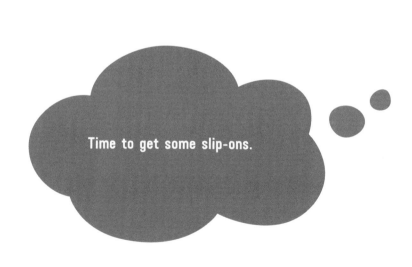

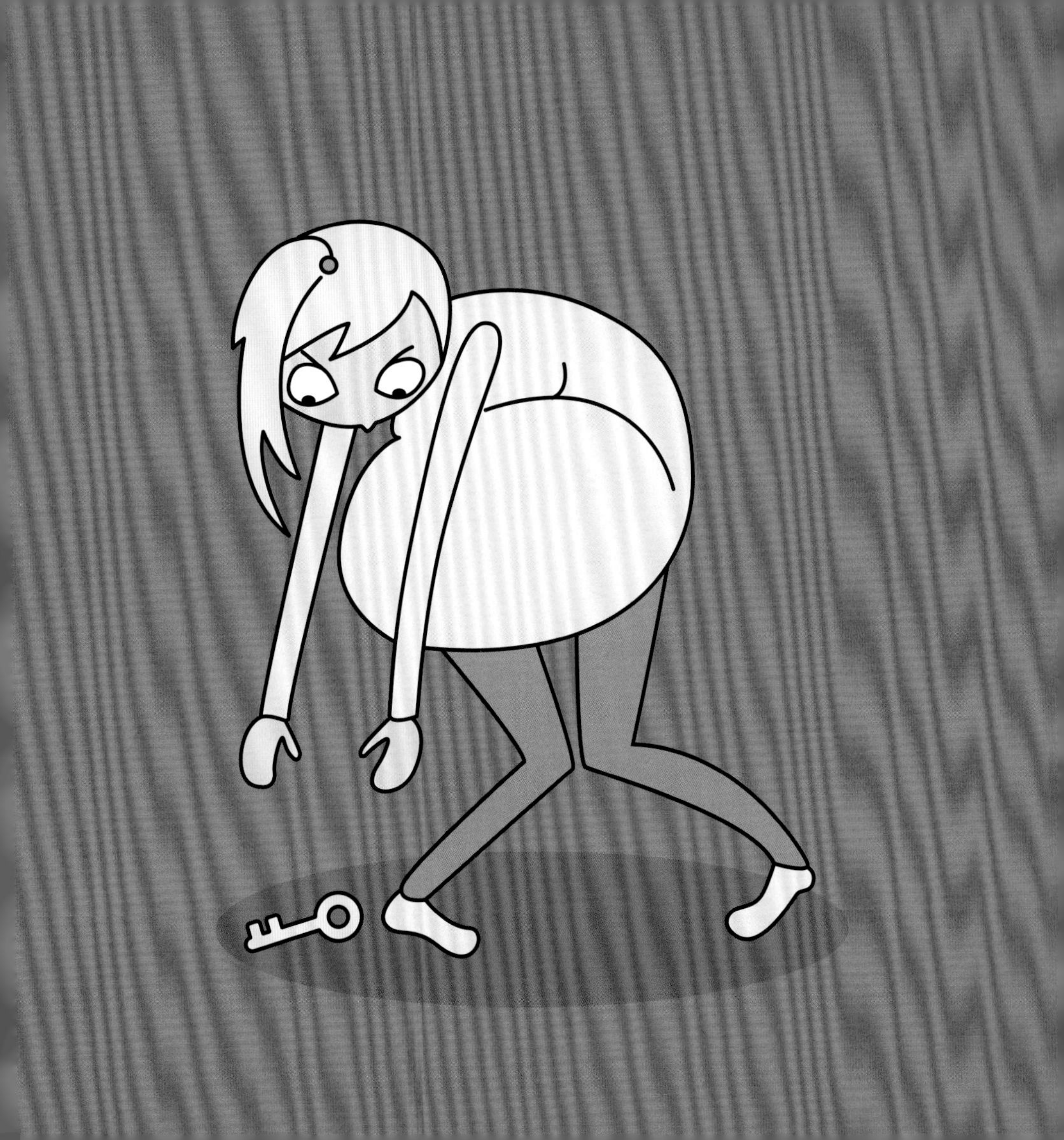

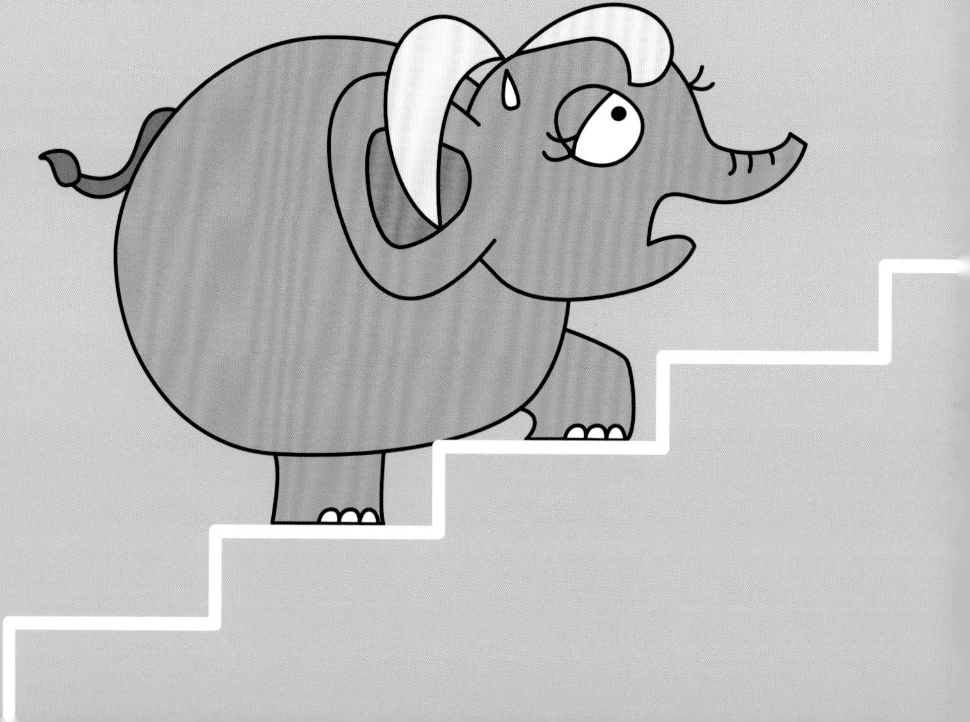

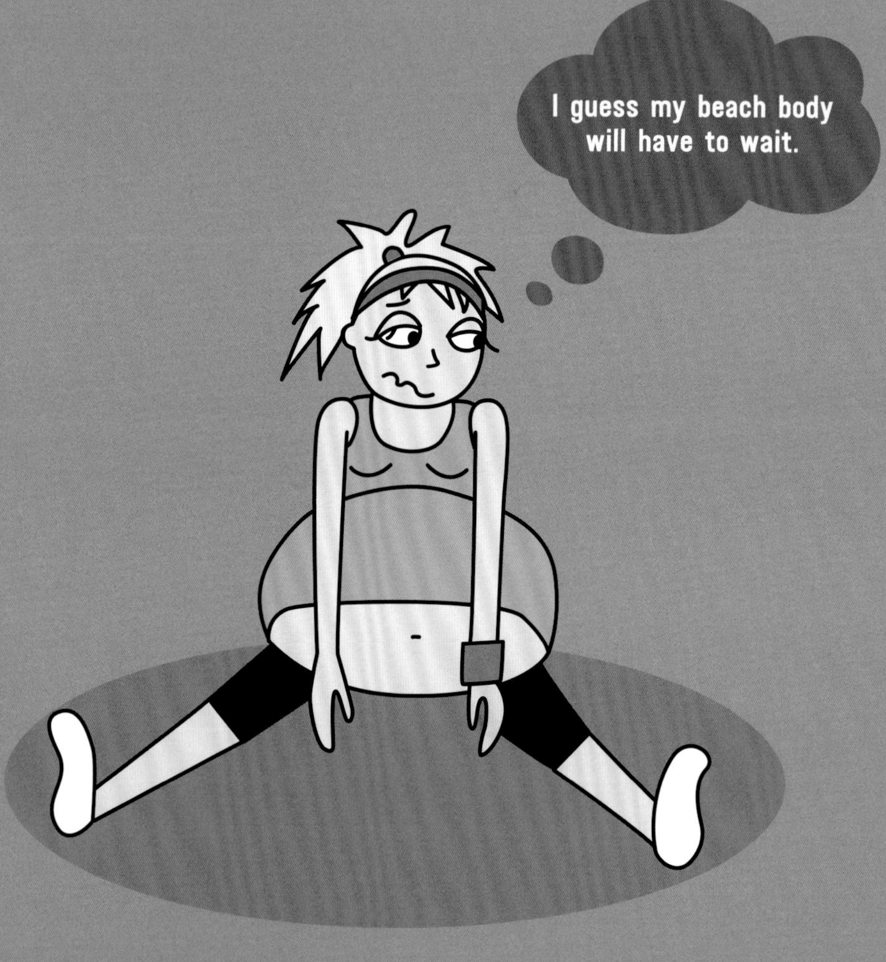
I guess my beach body will have to wait.

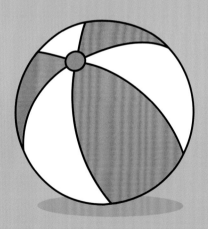

Free Willy!

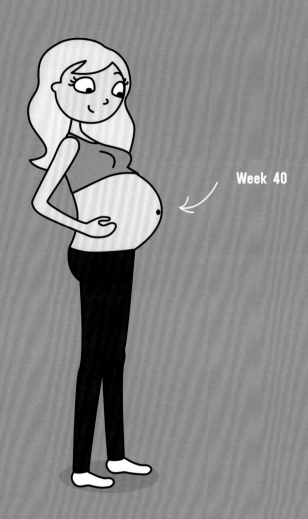

Week 40

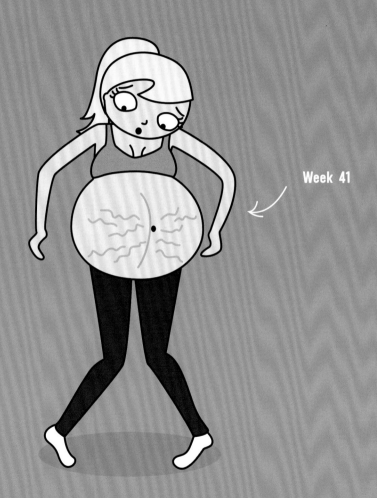

Week 41

Sometimes it's better to just keep your due date to yourself.

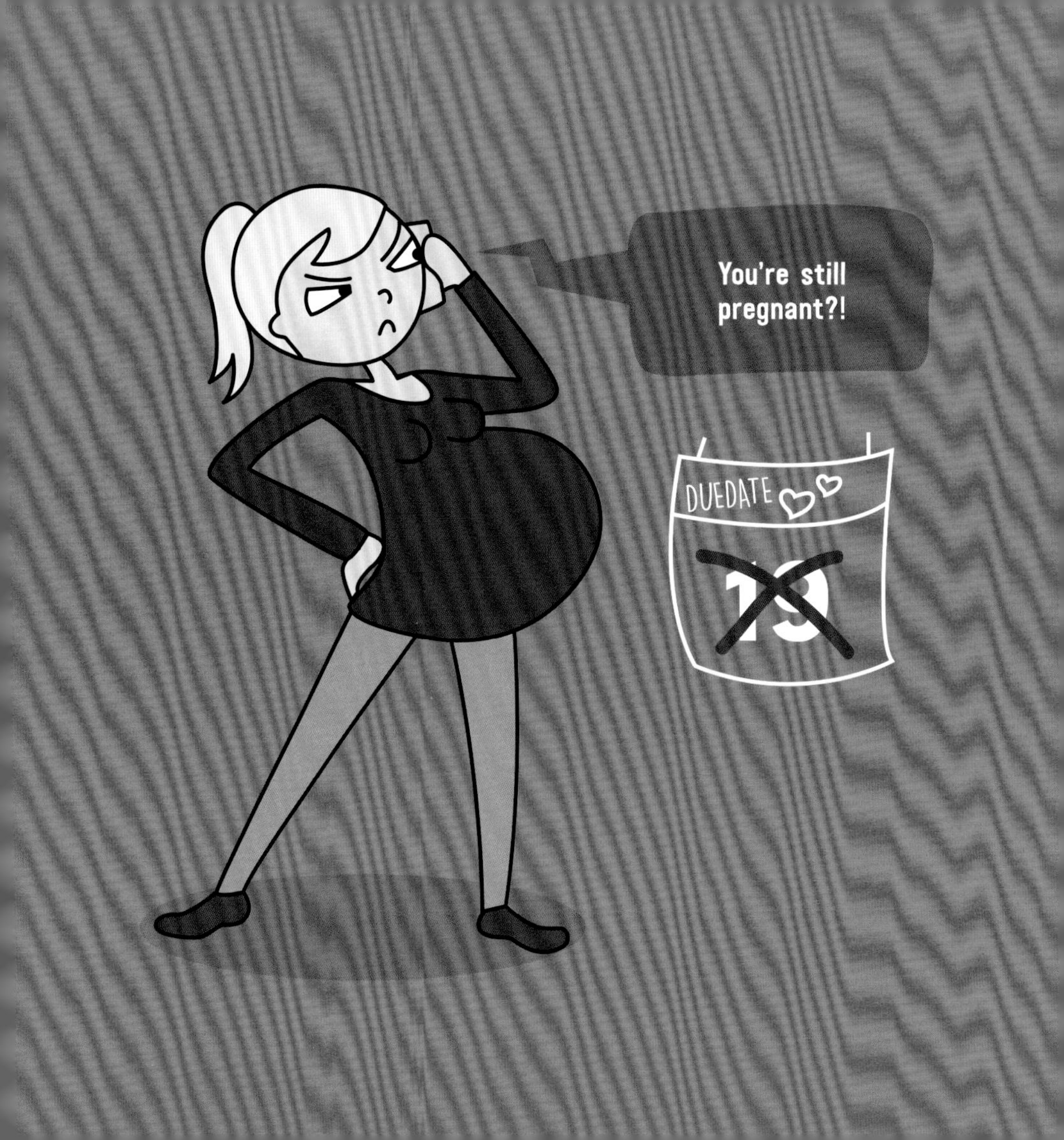
You're still pregnant?!
DUEDATE
19

Hey look, it's the mucus plug.

We're going to need some more chilies
to get this show on the road.

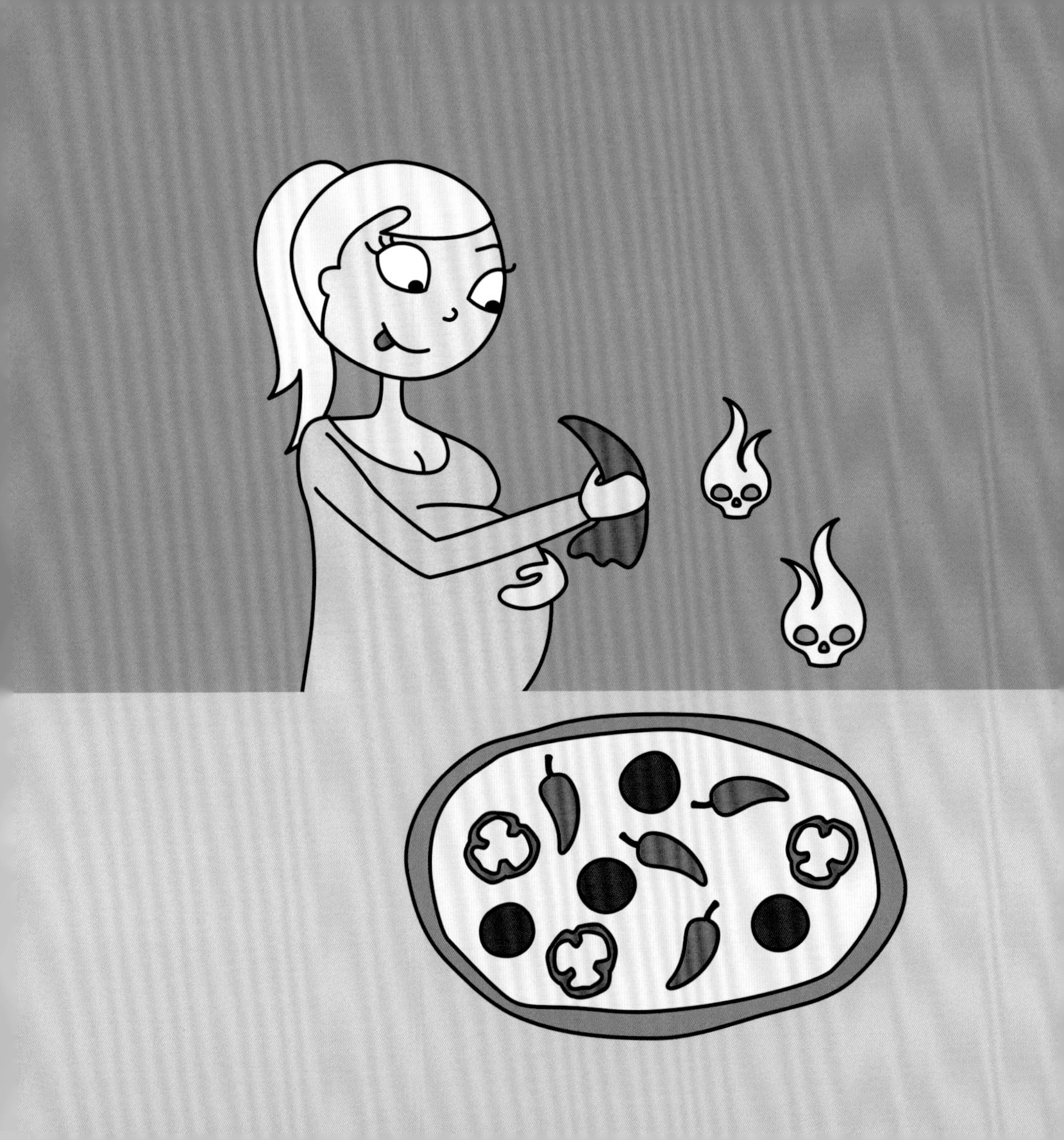

Couldn't you have at least waited until we got off the bus?

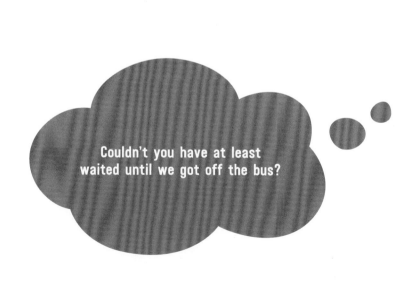

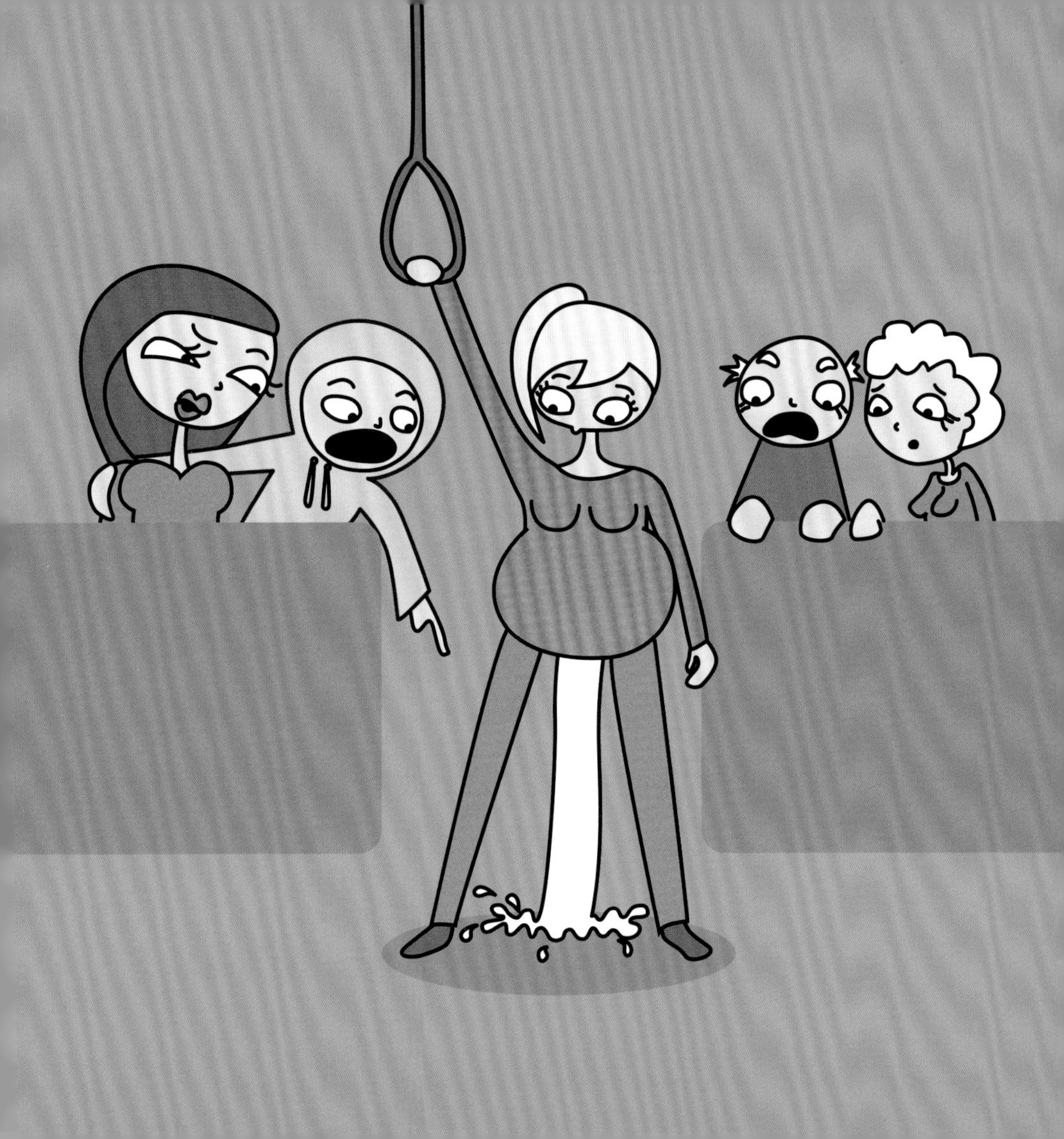

What I imagined giving birth to be like:

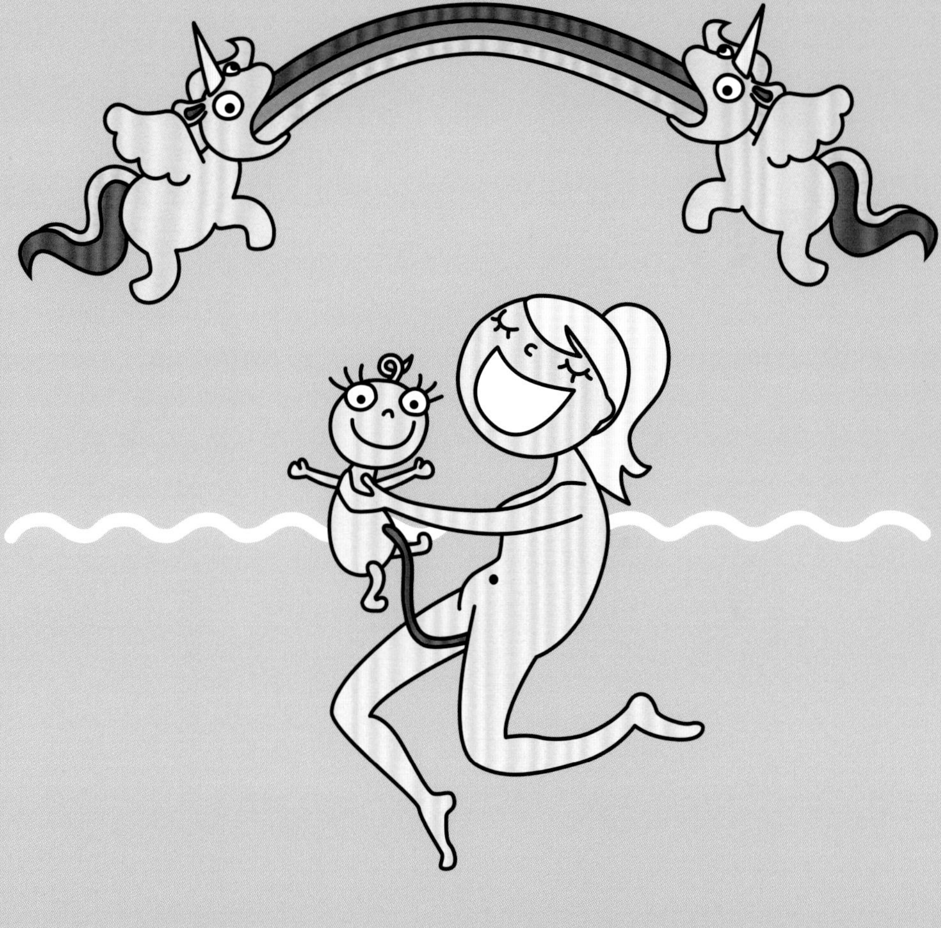

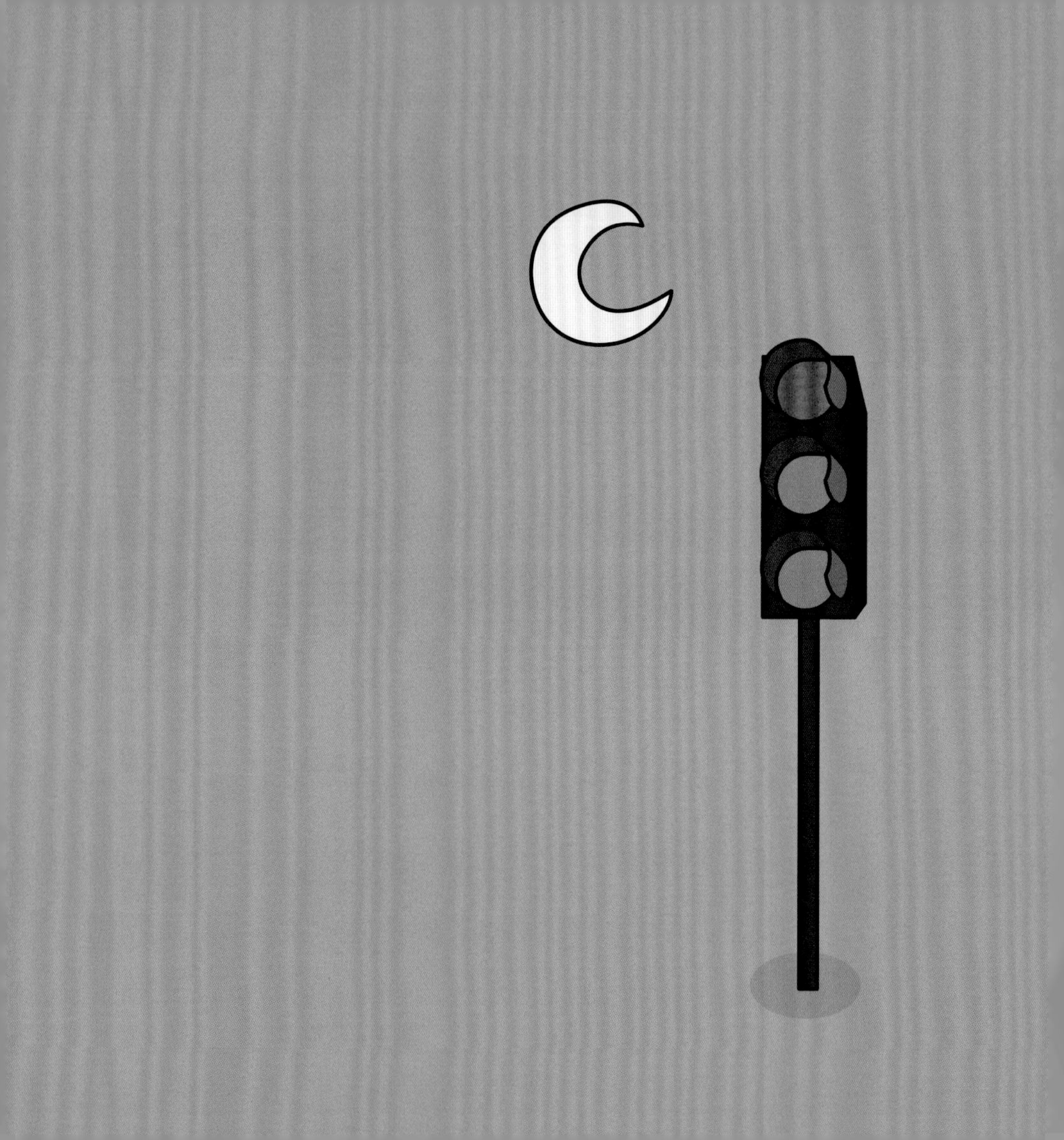

Stop complaining, it's just a little pain!

You did this to me!

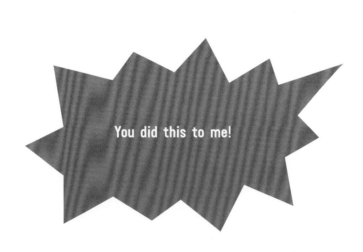

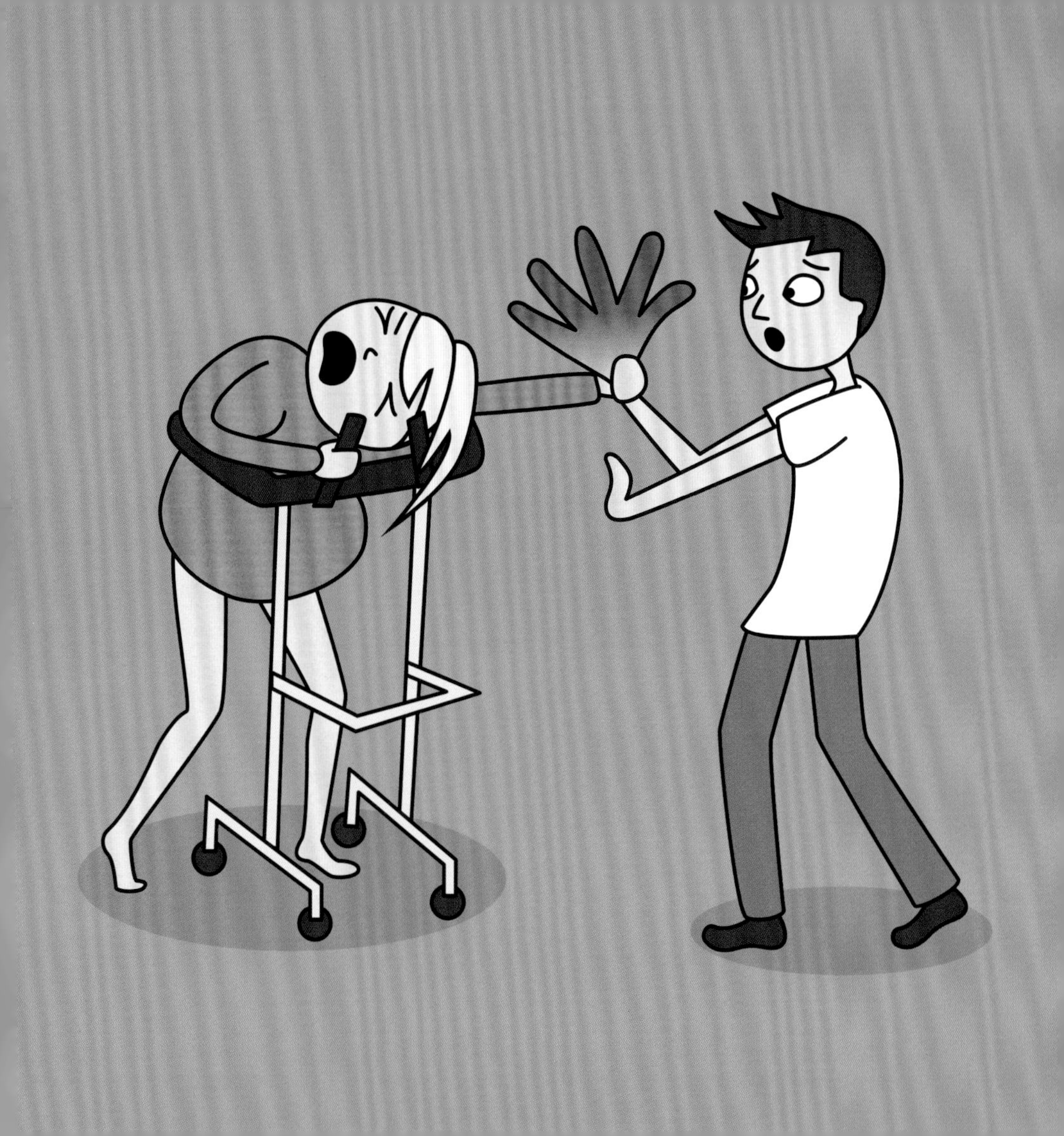

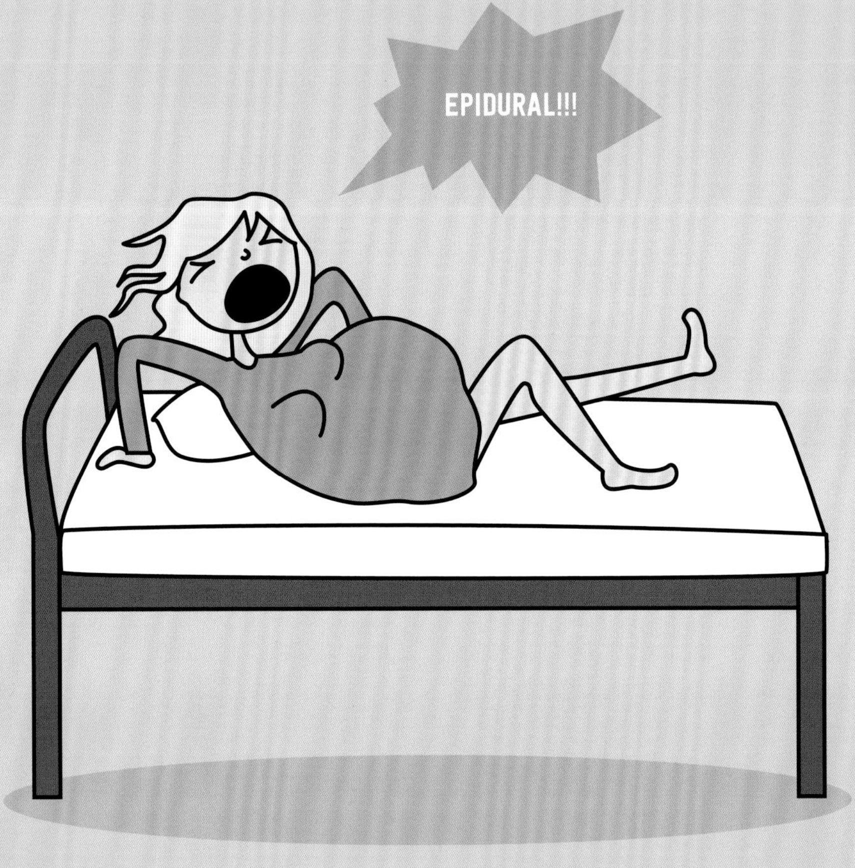
EPIDURAL!!!

Give me all you got!

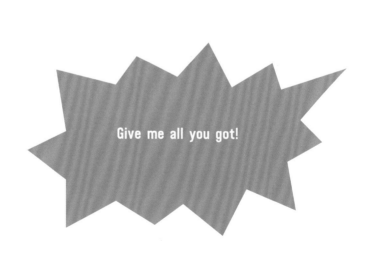

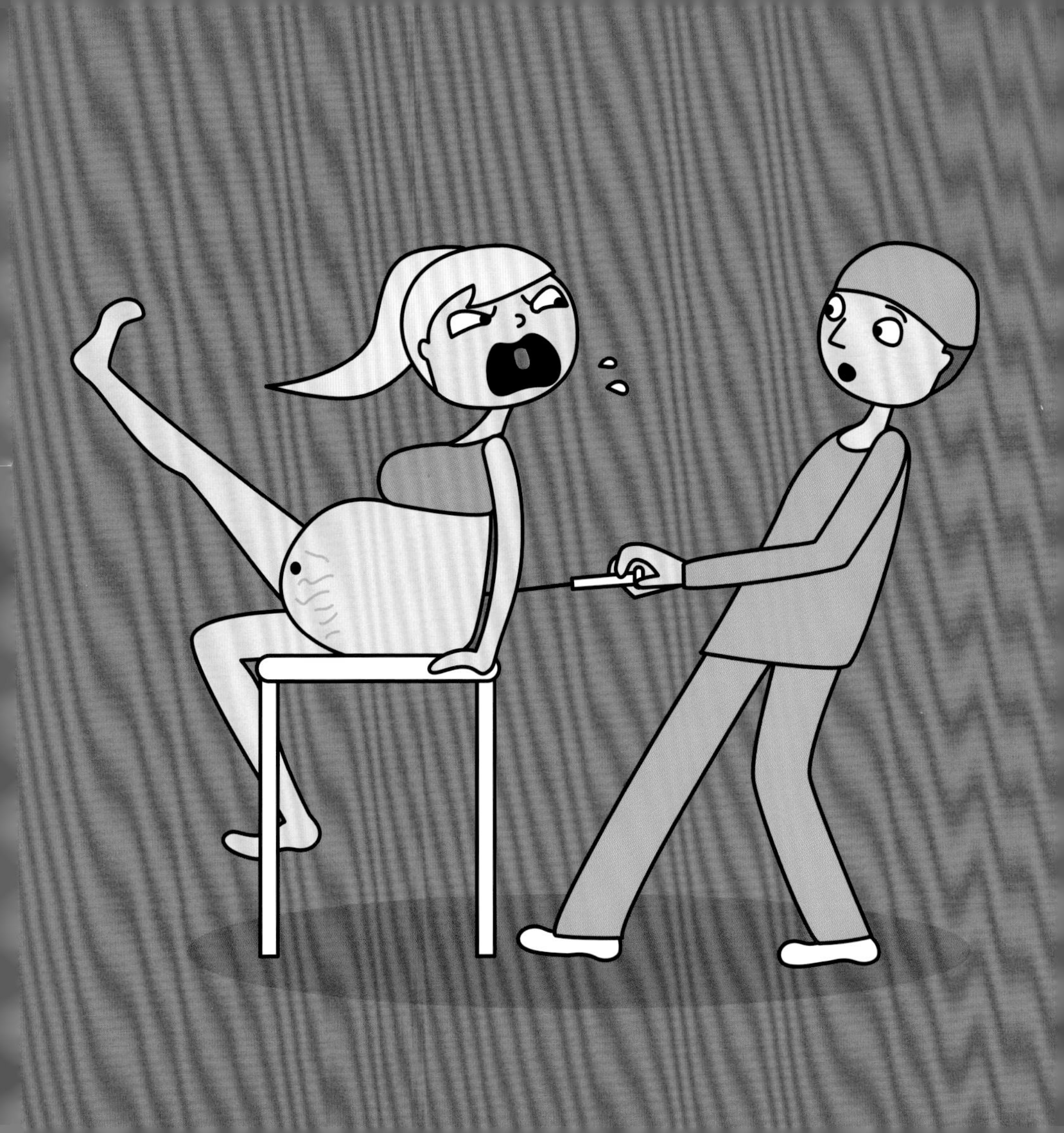

Best selfie ever.

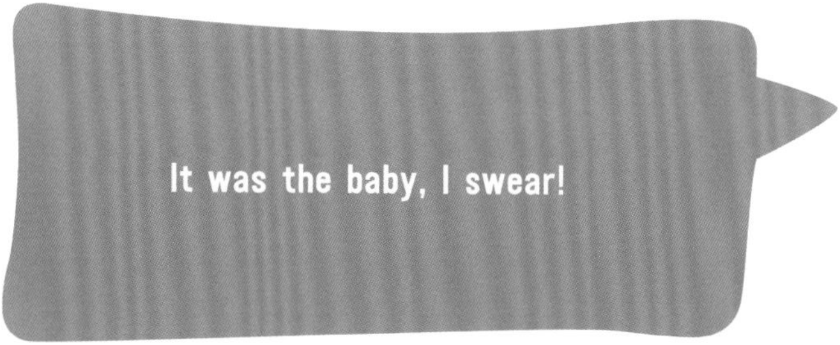
It was the baby, I swear!

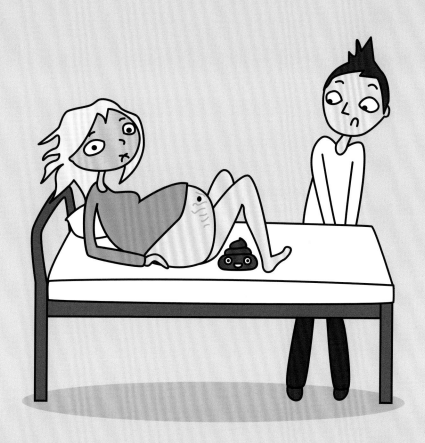

Hear me roar!

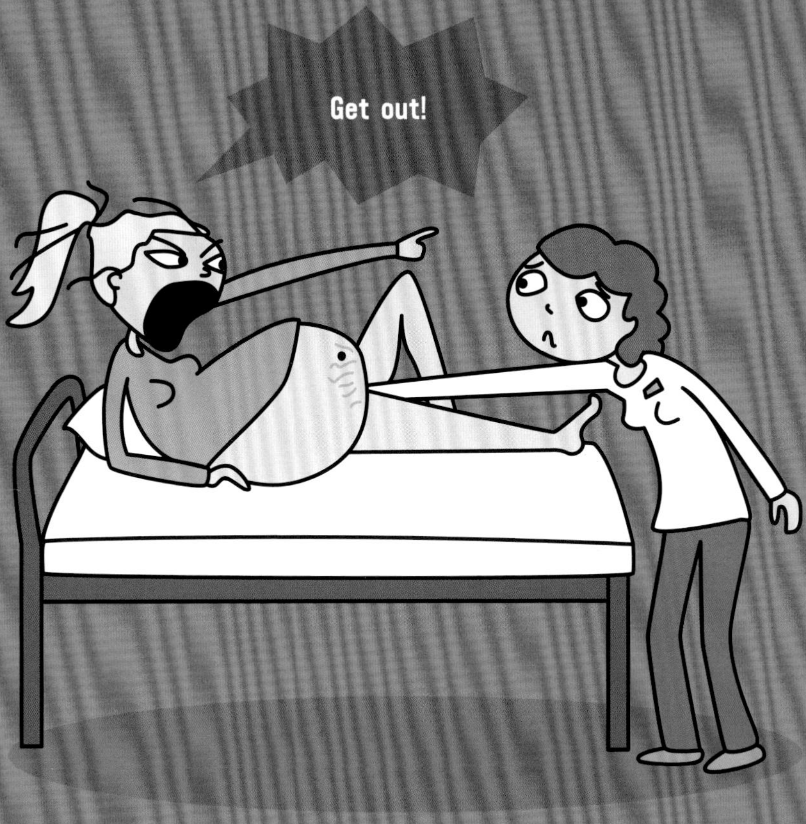
Get out!

Meet the new boss!

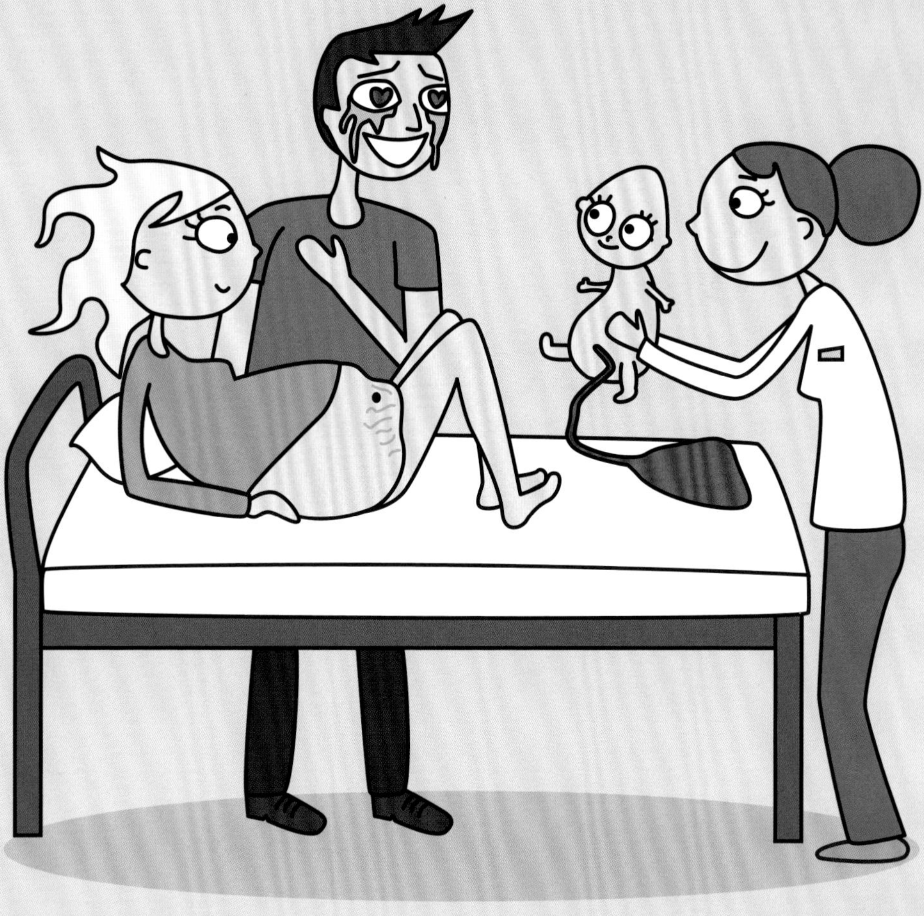

Pregnancy problems?
Can't remember any.

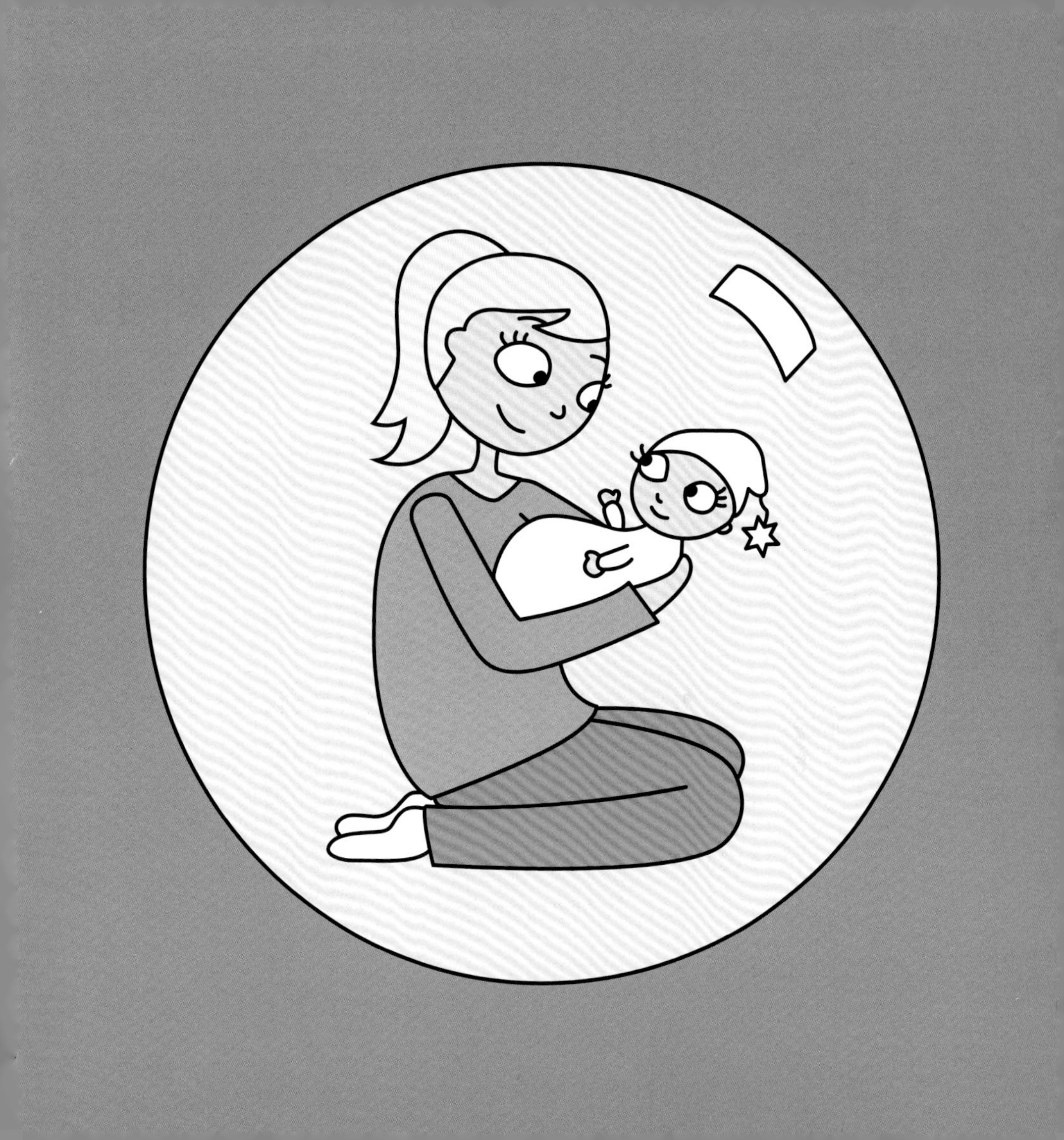